FROM SURVIVOR TO STRIVER

HOW GRATITUDE CAN TRANSFORM YOU INTO A SUPERHERO!

CHRIS DT GORDON

FROM SURVIVOR TO STRIVER

by Chris DT Gordon

Cover design and formatting by Bella Media Management

Printed in the United States of America for Worldwide Distribution.

Print ISBN: 979-8-9890237-0-7

ebook ISBN: 979-8-9890237-1-4

DISCLAIMER

AS I RECALL THE EVENTS in this book, I must acknowledge that several outside factors affected how well various circumstances played out for me. My relationships with my various family members and friends and their socio-economical advantages afforded me opportunities that others may not have had. Those advantages did not play a part in my choice to alter my mindset, though, and that is important to realize. You have the ultimate say on the choices you make!

ACKNOWLEDGMENTS

THROUGHOUT THE BOOK, I THANK several people who helped me along my journey. I mention some of those same people here, but I also include a few others who aren't mentioned in other places. However, this is not to say that I mention EVERYONE who offered me or my family assistance; if that were the case, this entire book would just be this section. If you did not see your name here, please know you have made me a better person with your love and support, and I apologize for the oversight.

First of all, I want to thank God for the blessings He has bestowed upon me. Throughout my hospital experience, I did all I could do, and I trusted the medical staff to do all that they could do. The rest was up to Him.

Becky, my wife, partner, and best friend, is an extremely close second on this list. She is the reason I'm writing this book. Without her love and support of me throughout this journey, I wouldn't have seen past my bandages and scarred, reconstructed body. She is, by far, my better 95%!

Jeff, my brother from the same mother, stepped up in a way I would never have requested of him. However, I'm not surprised that he did. He is an exemplary person, and I am better for being his sibling. Also, thanks for the iPad!

Michele, my older sister, wasn't able to offer the support others could at the time, but I know she did as much as she could, and I felt her love all the way from North Carolina.

While my own parents, Patricia and Frank Gordon, died long before I went into the hospital, I have thought of them hundreds of times as motivation to persevere on different projects and in certain situations. Although my own kids never knew them firsthand, it's my hope that Nana Pat and Papa Frank shine through my actions so their memories live on.

Bill and Dea, my parents by marriage ("in-laws" sounds impersonal to me), couldn't have welcomed me into their family more lovingly, and they were instrumental in helping our own family traverse the treacherous tides of my ordeal. From providing Becky, the kids, and Max the dog a place to stay for half a month to providing me with entertainment and post-discharge lodging to the inside joke of a certain prescription, Bill and Dea are true gifts from God. They also alerted their church, Trinity Lutheran in Rochester, to my situation, and Pastor Joel Haak and others kept me and the family in their prayers. Their love and support were also greatly appreciated.

To my stand-in parents Brenda and Dave, Sheila and "Big" Dave, Judy and "Coach" Carl: While I am not technically your son, you have always treated me like one, and I am all the better for it. Thank you for taking me and my family in and making sure we felt loved.

To my broFOMs (brothers from other mothers) John, Mark, Dave, Charlie, Jason, Phil, and Chris: Whether it was your physical or spiritual presence, your love and friendship made me smile even when the painkillers wore off. I'm so happy we've been able to connect and make more memories since 2015.

To my sisFOMs (sisters from other misters) Becky, Jill, Keri,

Beth, Kandice, Shawn, and Jamie: Thanks for letting your guys hang out with (or accompanying them to visit) me. Some of you helped me with this very book, while others, like Kandice, created artwork for my speaking business; you all mean a great deal to me!

To our New Ulm neighbors, friends, and law enforcement officers who helped us out in various ways while we were out of town: Thank you for protecting our house and assisting us with your time, talents, and treasure. We consider ourselves blessed to live in such a strong and caring community.

To my high school and college friends (especially my Theta Chi brothers), as well as my extended family members (both traditional family as well as my Messiah Lutheran Church family from Michigan): Thank you for helping out even if we hadn't connected in years or taking the time to check in with us. I deeply cherish our friendships!

To my colleagues who visited me in the hospital or sent well wishes and gifts to us (including a few of you even playing with my kids when they stayed in Rochester): I am truly blessed to be counted in your company and honored to be considered a peer of yours.

To the various medical professionals at Mayo Clinic and New Ulm Medical Center: Thank you for your professionalism, hard work, compassion, patience, and friendship. Not only would I not be here without you, I certainly wouldn't have accomplished what I have and will because of how you assisted me. Because of you, I can now help others in ways I didn't conceive before!

To my various teachers and coaches, including Master Esmaeil Torabpour and Mr. Barrett Stoll (Tae Kwon Do), Dan Faill, Jessica Gendron Williams, Clinton Young, Brendon Burchard, Jen Gottlieb, Chris Winfield, Rick Clemons, Corey Poirier, and many others (speaking), and Andrew Snow (running): Thank you for your tutelage and guidance as I work and strive to make the most of my second chance. You have certainly given this old dog new tricks to learn.

To my fellow NF (necrotizing fasciitis) survivors and their loved ones: Thank you for inspiring me to love and achieve as much as I can. I hope I do the same for you.

To my running friends, especially those in the New Ulm Run Club and the several Ragnar teams I've been honored to join: Thank you for your camaraderie, support, and challenges! I may run alone most days, but I greatly enjoy and fondly think about the excursions that I have with you.

To Carol Waltz, Kimberly King, Dea, Keri, Mark, and everyone else who helped me create this book: Thank you for your wisdom, insight, and guidance this past year; I certainly needed it. It is because of you that this work exists at all

Finally, to you, my old friend or new acquaintance: Whether you've helped me in the past or we are now meeting for the first time, thank you for taking this adventure with me! I view your time and future as extremely valuable commodities, and it is my fervent wish that I repay you for your investment with my story, message, and gratitude practices.

CONTENTS

INTRODUCTION

"It takes but one positive thought when given a chance to survive and thrive to overpower an entire army of negative thoughts."
—Robert H. Schuller

"Be the change that you wish to see in the world."
—Mahatma Gandhi

"Do or do not; there is no try."
—Yoda, *Star Wars Episode V: The Empire Strikes Back* (the best *Star Wars* movie)

OUR LIVES ARE A COLLECTION of thoughts and actions. We usually think of something to do, and then we do it. We think we're hungry, so we grab something to eat. We think of that REALLY witty comment, and then we let it rip with varying degrees of success.

Most of those thoughts aren't simply randomly firing synapses, though. They are often connected to an overlying attitude, also known as a mindset. What we do is often lined up with an agenda we have. For example, if we want to eat to feel good, we order the double cheeseburger and large fries. If, however, we are training for an athletic event, we might keep the portions small or even order something from the healthy side of the menu.

As I'll mention later in this book, "Where your thoughts go, your mind and body will follow." This statement works similarly to Beck's cognitive triangle[1]. For example, if I think about being a fast runner enough, I develop the mindset of a fast runner. From there, I start training to become faster. "Faster" is a subjective term because we all have different experiences and expectations. As I'm typing this sentence, I can run a 20-minute 5K. With the right mindset and training, I can conceivably run 1 ½ minutes faster. For someone with less experience running, a 20-minute 5K might seem out of reach; for others, 20 minutes is a snail's pace. It depends on the individual, and that's important to remember.

RUN YOUR OWN RACE.

Every person on the planet has their own set of experiences, even identical twins. Imagine a set of twins, identical in physical traits and ability. I'm thinking of Fred and George Weasley from the *Harry Potter* book series. Let's say they are training to make a professional Quidditch team. George suffers a serious injury to his dominant swinging arm one day and needs months to recover; Fred can spend that time training and improving his skills unabated. They now have separate experiences and different chances of making the professional team, even though George might recover and still look the same as Fred. (Note: I know that this scenario is not reflected in their actual story arcs, so please put down your wands.)

Like the Weasley twins, we all have different life experiences, thoughts, and viewpoints. That is immensely important to remember when we fall into the comparison trap. We see someone farther ahead on a certain path than we are, whether it's on social media, in our careers and interests, or literally in a race. We might become jealous and tempted to take actions that betray our own growth journey, like running faster to catch up with that person or abandoning our current strategy. Ultimately, though, our actions will betray us, and we'll end up on the side of the race course with our hands on our knees, gasping for breath (if we're lucky).

We also need to remember our journey is OUR journey and no one else's. President Teddy Roosevelt once stated, "Comparison is the thief of joy," and that is true. When we compare our accomplishments with others' achievements, we inevitably find ourselves lacking in at least one area, and that comparison can diminish the hard work and dedication we've demonstrated in our endeavors. As I trained to earn my BQ (Boston Marathon qualifying time), I didn't match up my weekly running mileage with that of Eliud Kipchoge, the current world record holder in the marathon. I didn't even compare my weekly input to that of my friend and veteran ultramarathoner John. I only looked at MY previous weekly mileage reports, and guess what I found. I had increased my weekly mileage by an average of over 50% by the end of the first phase of my training, I was running at least 6.55 miles every day aside from rest days, and I had improved the quality of my eating practices and sleep. I had become a much better runner, but I would've overlooked that realization if I worried about how I matched up against someone else.

As you read my story, please know that, by the time you finish the last page, I want you to become a better version of you and not to compare yourself to someone else. Is it egotistical of me to hope that my book makes you a better person? Perhaps. That hope is not borne out of pride or an inflated sense of self, though. Rather, my experience has made me a better person, and I want you to become your best version of you without needing to spend time in the hospital (that will make sense later).

WHAT'S AN ORIGIN STORY?

We all have an origin story, at least one to be certain. An origin story is a moment when you face a life-changing and/or threatening situation. You start asking yourself questions, and the thoughts that occupy your mind at that time start answering those questions. From there, you begin acting on those thoughts.

The term "origin story" is traditionally linked with comic books. Every superhero has one, even if they don't have powers. Captain Marvel can lift incredible amounts of weight, can fly at inhuman speeds, can survive the vacuum of space without a special suit, and can shoot energy blasts from her hands; Batman can't perform any of those feats, but his origin story is well-known throughout pop culture. An origin story is a life-changing event that challenges someone to make a choice that would change the trajectory of that person's life. Most people have several origin stories throughout their lifetimes, some more impactful than others.

I happen to be a comic book geek. I absolutely love comic book characters; the Teenage Mutant Ninja Turtles, One-Punch Man, Captain America, the Flash, and Nightcrawler are some of my favorites. My adoration for these modern-day Greek figures had remained steadily mild throughout high school and college, but as I am now more comfortable with myself, I have no problem letting others know that I like superheroes.

What is something that you really like? Congratulations! You're a geek about that topic. You can be a sports geek, a history geek, or a plumbing geek. The world is a beautiful place when everyone feels comfortable loving what they love and fearlessly letting others know about it.

"Where your thoughts go, your mind and body will follow."

This is the cornerstone of my message, but if you don't trust me, let's see what the Ivy League has to say. Many of us have experienced at least one occasion where a random billboard motivated us to take the next exit for some food. A 2009 study conducted by Yale University showed that unhealthy snacking amongst elementary-aged children consumed 45% more snacks when they were exposed to food-related advertisements while watching television, and some of the snack cravings were unconscious, meaning that the participants were unaware of the advertisements' influence[1]. When you think about something enough, it penetrates your mind and influences your actions. If those thoughts are positive, a positive mindset will likely develop and spawn positive actions. The same holds true for those negative thoughts.

A 2015 *Psychology.com* article by Laura M. Miele, PhD., entitled "The Effects of Psychology on Athletic Performance," illustrates the power of thought and how it affects physical performance. She writes that athletes who "visualize themselves having success will be successful." Further, she credits the acts of visualization and positive self-talk with having the ability to neutralize negative thoughts. Conversely, negative thoughts can lead to internal blocks (mindsets) that can then cause breaks in routines and even giving up on endeavors entirely[2]. It's also worth noting that studies have shown that thoughts and practices lead to forming habits. Some habits take less time to solidify than others, but a well-known 2009 study discovered that they take an average of 66 days to form[3].

Our minds are indeed the most powerful engines imaginable. How well they function, though, depends on the fuel we use. Keep that in mind as you learn more about me and my journey.

MY ORIGIN STORY

(or "The reason I wrote this book in the first place")

After 40 years of a pretty good life, my most epic origin story started; but first, some backstory. My wife Becky and I have three kids. We live in New Ulm, a small town of about 14,000 in south central Minnesota. I moved to Minnesota in 2002 from Michigan, where I was born and raised. I still consider myself a Michigander and automatically use the palm of my right hand as a map when people ask where I grew up. Every year we go to Michigan to visit my brother, other family members, and friends. I only eat Koegel's hotdogs; we either load up on them when we're in Michigan, or we order them online. I refer to the University of Michigan as the only "U of M." I drink pop and bake with soda.

So why do I live in Minnesota if I'm such a Michiganstan? I love Becky more.

Becky and I are both teachers. She teaches Social Studies at the local high school, and I am a veteran middle school special education teacher for a public online school. In fact, I've been teaching online since 2012 (yes, LONG before the COVID pandemic). Our children are all athletic nerds. They all love to learn, perform on stage, and geek out on *Harry Potter* and Weird Al Yankovic.

OK, back to the origin story. On Wednesday, March 18, 2015, while Becky and the kids were preparing to leave for school and daycare, I picked up two-year-old Seth (one of a pair of twins) and flew him to the garage, swaying him back and forth. I misjudged my distance from the garage wall and accidentally scraped the back of my right hand against it. It barely bled, so I put Seth into the van, kissed everyone goodbye, waved them off, and went into the house. I washed my wound as well as I could, put antibiotic cream and a bandage on it (my usual response to cuts), walked into my home office, and started my workday.

On Saturday I woke up to discover a red, lacrosse ball-sized bump on my right elbow. Becky and I had gone bowling the night before with her teaching colleagues; did I awkwardly torque my elbow trying to get that 5-10 split? Regardless of its cause, I drove myself to the walk-in clinic at the local hospital. The attending doctor replied that it could have been bursitis (an inflammation of the bursa sac in our joints), that I should keep an eye on it, and I should come back if the situation changes.

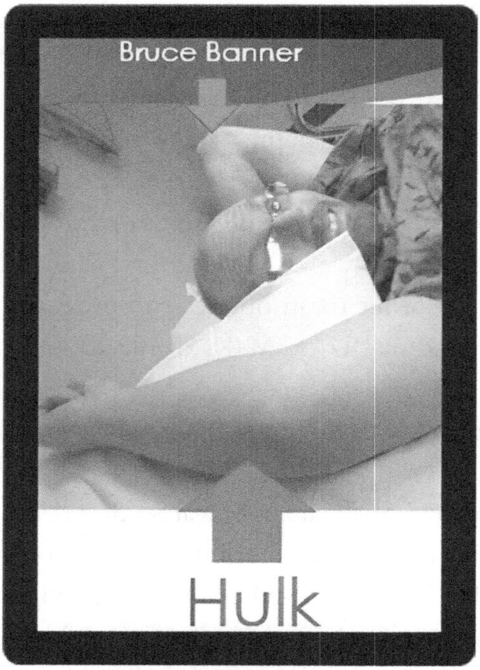

Ten hours later, I came back.

The red bump on my elbow had spread throughout my arm, shoulder, chest, and back. I looked like the Incredible Hulk in mid-transformation. Additionally, I was extremely lethargic and slightly nauseous. I did still have my quirky sense of humor intact, as evidenced by the picture I asked Becky to take that displays both my puny Banner arm and the Hulk Smash arm.

What was less humorous was the sepsis that spread throughout my body.

The nurse couldn't obtain an accurate blood pressure reading on me. At the time, I didn't think too much of it as I was overly occupied with my ginormous right arm. Later, I researched the effects of sepsis.

I'm happy I was ignorant at that time.

Put simply, sepsis is the body's overreaction to an infection. It tries to kill the invading object, but it sometimes leads to disastrous results for the host, such as organ failure. Inflammation from an infection can cause dangerously low blood pressure, and an infected person can die in as little as 12 hours. Imagine that you ask your child to pick up a toy off the floor, and instead of throwing a simple tantrum, the child burns the house down: That's sepsis. It can essentially kill you as it tries to save you.

Again, all of this came from a simple scratch: Something that had happened hundreds of times before with no horrible side effects.

The medical staff kept me overnight for obvious reasons. On Sunday morning the attending doctor approached me and said that they could not do anything else for me; my problem was beyond them. She followed up by asking me where I wanted to go. I immediately said, "Mayo (Clinic in Rochester, MN)."

Few hospital systems exist where you can identify them by one or two words alone. Mayo is the Prince or Beyoncé of healthcare providers. The Midwest healthcare giant is world-renowned for their wide-ranging medical expertise and list of high-profile patients. Saudi Arabian royalty have made their presence known in Rochester beginning in 2009 when they require top notch medical care. So, telling the doctor that I wanted to go there was a no-brainer. Plus, Bill and Dea, Becky's parents, lived 10 minutes from the hospital;

Bill was even one of the hospital's chaplains. That way, Becky, the kids, and Max the dog could stay someplace safe and familiar (and free) for the few days I would be there.

Certainly, this would only take a few days.

Right?!

After I called Becky to let her know about the move to Rochester, the medical staff wheeled my gurney to an ambulance, whisked me away to the municipal airport, and strapped me tightly to the gurney which was then latched to the inside of the cabin of a Cessna-style airplane (they would've used a helicopter, but a snowstorm was quickly approaching). After 20 minutes of practically kissing the cabin wall, we landed in Rochester, and I was wheeled to another ambulance and taken to St. Mary's Hospital, the largest hospital within Mayo.

Once I arrived there, my recollection of events started to get fuzzy. I vaguely remember seeing Becky and Bill as I entered the hospital, and the next thing I recall is having a surreal conversation with Dr. Mark Morrey, the surgeon who would end up performing my first operation. I was seated in a wheelchair, and my head swayed back and forth. Apparently, Dr. Morrey informed me that I had contracted necrotizing fasciitis (flesh-eating bacteria), and they would start removing the infected skin and underlying tissue. While my memory of the conversation is not lucid, I do recall being rather gung-ho and jokey about the whole situation, saying that I was "ready to go" and "Let's do this!" My behavior weirded Dr. Morrey out a bit; he was used to people in my situation being scared, weepy, and more concerned for their lives, not cocky and jovial while in a drugged stupor.

That's the last thing I remember before my surgeries.

At the time of my first surgery, the infection had encompassed my right arm, shoulder, chest, and back. Doctors used a red marker to track its progress as they were preparing me for upcoming procedures. They employed a similar technique to how firefighters battle a forest fire: They marked lines ahead of the trouble spots so they would be sure to completely remove the infection. When the red marker line touched the base of my neck, Becky left the room, overwhelmed with sadness and concern.

Despite my dire situation, God wasn't ready to take me Home just yet; that said, I wasn't quite out of the woods. Becky was told before my second surgery that they were going to amputate my right arm. No question. The infection had progressed so deep into my forearm that they thought that it couldn't be saved. However, the attending occupational therapist noticed that I still had hand function, so they removed a 15" by 4" flap of skin from my left thigh (that included part of an artery) and attached it to the back of my hand and forearm. Since it's my thigh on my hand, I call that flap my "thand;" I might copyright that term at some point.

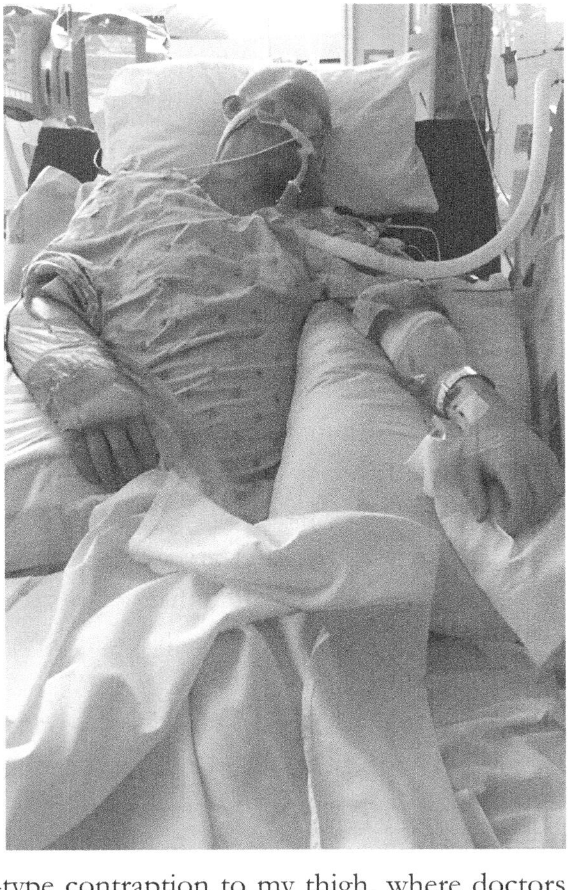

Since I had a 60-square inch section of skin extracted from my left thigh and large runner/soccer player thighs, doctors could not close the wound without making physical alterations. So, they removed an entire thigh muscle from my left quadricep. Then they attached a double knob and shoestring-type contraption to my thigh, where doctors gradually tightened the knobs, which activated the "shoestrings" to close the wound. The process lasted a couple weeks and ultimately left a 15-inch scar. To this day, my left thigh looks like a stuffed duffel bag, aside from the dent where the scar exists.

When a significant portion of your torso is filleted, you need numerous skin grafts to cover that area. Thankfully, my thighs and back were ready to serve! The surgeons used a skin graft harvester (imagine a comically large cheese slicer) to remove over two dozen slices of my sweet, sweet ivory goodness and placed them all over the infected areas, which were already covered with foundational material called Integra that helped the skin grafts take hold more securely. Fun fact about skin graft harvesting sites: They do not fully heal, so it looks like I had a horrendous waxing mishap. Being a ginger isn't the only reason why I don't tan now.

MY "NEW" REALITY

When I awoke from my drug-induced coma, I was at the bottom of a water slide, engulfed in a huge cast, immobilized by a thigh brace, and being pummeled by gallons of green water. You likely have two questions after reading that last sentence:

1) When did they start installing water slides in hospitals?

Answer: Never. I was hallucinating while throwing up after waking from the coma.

2) Why was the water green?

Answer: It was the fluid that doctors used to take CT scans of my body as I was out. Actually, that fluid isn't even green. That's just what I imagined.

I was, to say the least, not pleased to find myself in that scenario. I roared in confusion and frustration, scaring a poor nurse; I really should have apologized to her. My brother Jeff, who had traveled from Michigan to help Becky and the kids, almost jumped back on the plane after seeing my tirade. Thankfully, he did not. Instead, he called Becky and Bill to let them know I was awake. He also gave me an iPad that, coincidentally, still works as I'm writing this years later. The three of them expressed their happiness and relief with seeing me awake and didn't offer me much more information. They wanted me to get my rest and not worry about anything.

Easier said than done.

I spent that first night drifting in and out of sleep, adjusting to my new body. My right arm was covered in a gigantic yellow cast that exposed most of my fingers, but my pinky was covered. More than once I imagined (read: hallucinated) that it had been amputated and I could perhaps receive a "robopinky." I would return to the traditional classroom and use my mechanical digit as a laser pointer. How cool would that be?!?

Spoiler alert: I did not get a robopinky.

To this day, my recollections of my first post-coma day are pretty fuzzy, though I clearly remember two details, one of which blew my mind.

Becky visited me early that next morning and was chatting with me and the medical staff members who were coming in and out of my hospital room. During one conversation I asked someone why a medical staff member wasn't available on a Monday (or Tuesday; the previous night was REALLY long).

Becky looked at me incredulously and said, "Chris, it's Friday."

"FRIDAY?!" I exclaimed. "It's Friday?!? How can it be Friday?!?"

It turned out that performing all of those surgeries I mentioned above took several days. (Note: You may have realized that fact when you first read about the surgeries, but I was obviously oblivious.) After a few minutes of repeating the word "Friday" to the dismay of Becky and the present medical staff, I started formulating plans for that second recollection.

Before I fell ill, some colleagues and I had been planning for our Mid-Year Talent Show, which was held at a community center in the Minneapolis/St. Paul Twin Cities area. Over 20 student groups signed up, and I had even written a teacher skit. Performing colleagues had even attended online rehearsals.

Why am I explaining all this? Well, not only had I written and directed the teacher performance, but I was slated to emcee the talent show and perform in a student skit, and it was all happening THAT VERY DAY! I started formulating a plan where Becky would drive me to the talent show which was about 100 miles away, and I would still emcee the show and direct the skit from the comfort of a wheelchair. It wouldn't be that hard, and she could even bring me right back to the hospital when the show was over.

She spared me the embarrassment of not laughing in my face (as far as I recall), but she repeatedly denied my request. During her refusal, I was enlightened to the fact that, among the numerous procedures performed on me, I also had a catheter attached to my nether regions. No wonder I didn't feel the need to go to the bathroom! I kept hoping throughout the day that I could break away to Chaska until, finally, I cast my gaze upon the hospital room clock as it struck 5:00PM.

"Well, the talent show is starting," I lamented before throwing up into a bag.

A couple days later, Erin, one of my colleagues sent me a video where the entire talent show audience wished me well. It was almost like attending the event itself, and I didn't even need to wear pants (thanks to the catheter).

The next week was a blur of hallucinations, surgeries, room changes, and more hallucinations. Seriously, if you absolutely need to know about the hallucinations, just skip ahead right now! I remember being in good spirits, but I still had a great deal of uncertainty about how/if I was going to recover. That uncertainty led to what I call "personal bacteria."

While the surgeons masterfully removed every bit of flesh-eating bacteria from my body, I was now experiencing an onset of "personal bacteria:" Questions that were invading my mind to which I had no answers. They revolved around my future. What would I be able to do once/if I fully recovered? At that moment, I had already undergone several bouts of reconstructive surgery. I was wearing an enormous yellow cast that encapsulated my right arm and shoulder (though it felt like I was carrying it) and protected areas of my body that had been fileted. Two knobs flanked a wide chasm in my left thigh, one which forced doctors to extract a quadricep muscle so the wound could close. I had been told that doctors would soon start stripping layers of skin from my back and thighs that would cover those exposed parts of the right arm, shoulder, and torso. A couple weeks prior, I had run a Pi Day race (3.14 miles) in 19 minutes and 29 seconds, averaging 6:12/mile; now I had a gaping hole in my left leg and was missing an entire muscle. In my life I had only spent one night in the hospital, and that was when Becky gave birth to our oldest child. Now, doctors were informing Becky that they were hopeful I could feed myself with my right arm.

I also worried about my mental stability. Doctors informed Becky that, at one point, I had a 30% chance of survival, and while that percentage had risen, I certainly wasn't out of the woods. They had discussed the possibility of post-traumatic stress disorder (PTSD) and depression. As my body was healing from extensive reconstructive surgery, I was receiving very powerful pain medications; among those was Ketamine. Ketamine not only helped me manage my pain exceptionally well (I was thankfully physically numb for most of my first few post-surgery weeks), but it also supplied me with some mind-altering hallucinations. I'll talk about those trippy experiences later, I promise. Suffice it to say, though, they messed with my mind. Becky repeatedly corrected or reminded me of the reality of several situations. Would the rest of my life be like that? How would I react when I scratched myself again? How would I relate to Becky and the kids? My friends and colleagues? Absolute strangers?

Then there was the cost of my hospitalization. Becky's school supplied us with a great insurance package, but how much of my recovery would be covered? Also, I did not have many personal time off (PTO) days from my own school; how much money would we lose from lost wages? Would I be able to continue teaching after my hospitalization?

I always considered myself a reasonably positive person. Throughout my life, I've dealt with family deaths, bullying, betrayal, and other negative experiences that tested me…but nothing like this. This was nothing anyone I knew had encountered. With no frame of reference, my mindset headed south.

ENTER TAG

LUCKILY, THOUGH, THE TRIP DOWN to Negativeville didn't last long.

Becky visited me at least once a day during the first two weeks of my hospitalization. During one of those visits, she told me about how various people in our lives were stepping up to help us. Our neighbors snow blowed our driveway and shoveled our walkways; thanks neighbors! Friends and colleagues who lived in the Rochester area not only stopped by Bill and Dea's house to see how the family was doing, but many also donated food, toys, and clothes to the kids and played with them. (As it turns out, Becky, the kids, and Max the dog ended up staying in Rochester for two entire weeks.) She also told me that, as soon as she informed my brother Jeff that I had contracted necrotizing fasciitis, he found the first flight from Grand Rapids, MN to Minneapolis and then found a shuttle to Rochester, stayed a week and a-half (sometimes even sleeping at the hospital to get the latest updates on my condition), AND bought me an iPad so I could distract myself while I recovered in my hospital room.

As Becky finished telling me all this information, I experienced a unique feeling. When I speak to audiences, I describe it as the washing away of that "personal bacteria." I also compare it to the bat flying through Bruce Wayne's window, inspiring him to become Batman.

That epiphany is what I now call "The Attitude of Gratitude" (TAG). All those acts of love and kindness Becky mentioned flipped a switch in my head. Those unanswered questions that led to potential negativity and despair left my mind, and new questions filled that void.

SO MANY THINGS TO COUNT!

The first question was "What good things do I have in my life?" As expected, my mind immediately went to "the big things:" My faith, my family, my friends, my home, and my job. Each of them played such a huge role in my life on a daily basis; I wouldn't be the same person without them.

After a moment, though, I started wondering about "the smaller things:" Those seemingly insignificant parts of my life that made me smile, helped me accomplish a task, or just made my life even a little bit easier. As I began thinking about those items, I realized how much wealth I truly had around me. I couldn't sell those items for much on eBay, mind you, but I saw the value of the items in my possession.

Around the time of my revelation, the first season of the Marvel show *Daredevil* premiered on Netflix. I downloaded the Netflix app onto my new iPad and quickly found myself engrossed in the trials of Matt Murdock (Trials, get it? Because he's a lawyer and… nevermind.). I fondly remember binging episodes during my mornings between my nursing visits and occasionally on those nights before a surgery. Many people consider that first season one of the best Marvel productions to date, but I will always see it as something much more special.

I also thought about my hospital room window. It was about 10 feet away from my hospital bed, and even in the middle of the day, the sun never shined in my eyes when I was bedridden. When you are stationery for an extended period of time, you are dependent on others for just about everything. The fact that I didn't have to ask anyone to close the shades was a blessing.

Then there's the hospital pizza. As I have spoken to audiences, podcast hosts, and others over the years, I have found that, by and large, hospital food does not have an overly favorable reputation. Various opinions have usually ranged from "alright" to "horrible."

Once I was able to eat solid food, I ordered a personal pizza. Even before I took the first bite, I knew it would be good. Then I took a bite...and realized how hot it was! I spit out the piece and sucked down some protein shake to quench the fire torching the roof of my mouth. After a few minutes, I took another bite...and fell in love! It was a deep dish with just enough spice and tanginess in the sauce. There is a chance I might have favored it because I hadn't had pizza for a month at that time, but I still ordered it numerous times during my hospitalization, and I enjoyed it every time.

The more I thought about the various things in my life that I appreciated, the more I found value all around me. The computers I regularly used, the toothbrush I reached for each morning and evening, the food I ate every day, materials used to hold our house together, my various fandoms...all those things helped me to complete work, keep me happy, keep my family warm and safe. I even considered items I barely used like tools (I am not mechanically inclined), and I immediately felt thankful that I owned them.

SO MANY PEOPLE TO THANK!

After thinking about WHAT I appreciated in my life, my mind transitioned to considering WHOM I appreciated in my life. Again, when thinking of answers for such a question, our minds usually gravitate to our closest and longest lasting social circles: Family, friends, those who share our faith or belief systems, neighbors, colleagues/classmates, etc. That certainly happened to me, with the numerous blessings Becky, Bill, Dea, Jeff, my other family members and friends, and others had bestowed upon me.

Becky, of course, jump started my move into greater gratitude, successfully ran the household (with some occasional help), AND taught four days a week; her school allowed her to take Fridays off so she could bring the kids to Rochester to see me over the weekends.

Bill and Dea invited Becky and the kids (again, a six-year-old and twin toddlers) into their house for two solid weeks and just about every weekend afterwards for two months, visited me several times a week, and kept my spirits high through, among other things, playing Scrabble on an iPad and getting frequent Subway deliveries.

Jeff, as I mentioned before, flew to Minnesota from Michigan as soon as he learned about my situation, took a shuttle from the Twin Cities airport to Rochester, stayed in Minnesota for a week-and-a-half, and bought me the iPad. He would occasionally even sleep overnight at the hospital so he could get the latest news on my condition. Later on, he and HIS Becky, and their daughter Hope drove over from Michigan to see us for the Memorial Day weekend. Yes, I said HIS Becky; we both married Beckys. When we're all together, my wife goes by Becky Ann or Minnesota Becky, and his wife goes by Becky Kay or Michigan Becky. (It's slightly pathetic how amused he and I are by just saying "Becky" hearing them both respond).

MY Becky's and my colleagues stepped in to help in various ways. Joe, a retired Social Studies teacher and friend, taught in Becky's place on Fridays so she could visit me each weekend with confidence that the content would be delivered consistently. Some of my online colleagues who lived in the Rochester area stopped by Bill and Dea's to donate food, clothing, and toys to the kids, play with them, and offer their support in other ways. One of my colleagues recorded a heartwarming video of people at that talent show wishing me a speedy recovery. Colleagues from both schools even stopped by my hospital room to visit me. Those I clearly remember include Kelsy, Erin, Justin, both Michelles, Mahria, Staci and Connor, and even a student and his family who traveled over two hours to see me. (Again, if I forgot anyone, I apologize.) Pastor Bode, the pastor from our church, called from time to time to check up on me, and Pastor Bernau from our sister congregation stopped by and delivered cards that some kids made for me. Some of my high school classmates, including Courtney, Heather, and Jackie, sent me and my family fun toys and other geeky items, including a Han Solo in Carbonite beach towel that is always fun to lay out on the sand.

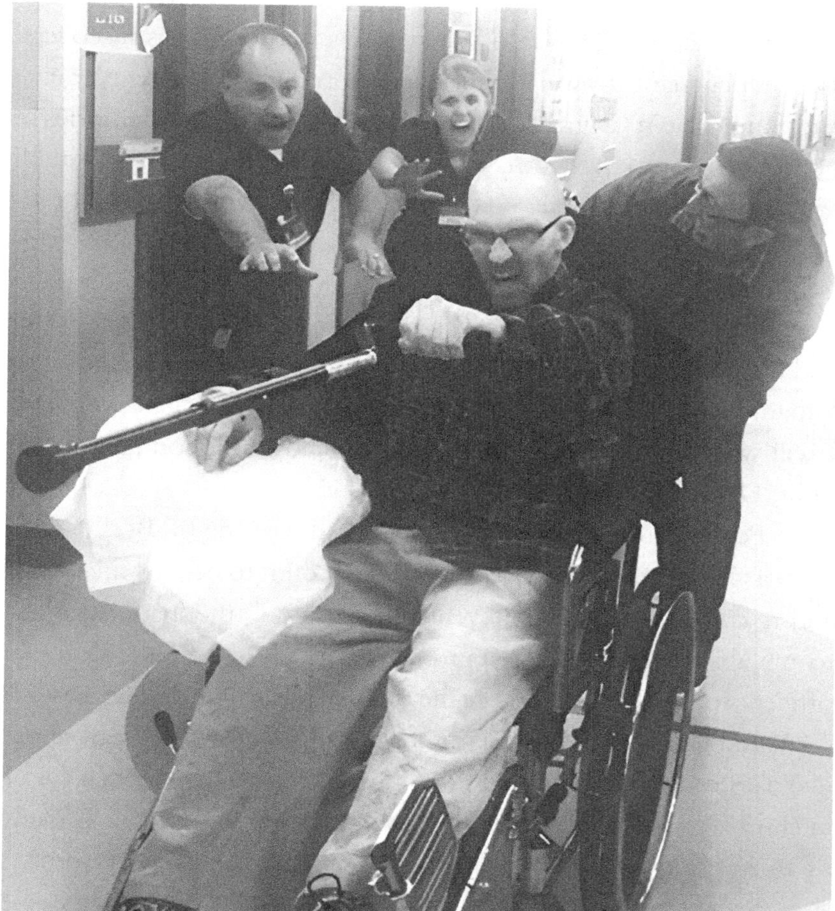

Dave and Beth, my best friend from my fraternity and his wife (whom I also met in college), flew in from Montana to spend a weekend with me. They even took me and Bill out to a local restaurant for dinner. It was my first time off-campus; I was so excited! Dave helped me "escape" from two of my nurses. He wheeled me to Bill's vehicle, we drove to the restaurant...and I lasted 45 minutes. I was so overwhelmed and exhausted from the ordeal that I could only handle three bites of my bean burger. For some reason, I thought a bean burger would go down easier than a real one. I was wrong.

That wasn't the first memory of Dave that I have from that weekend excursion, though. When we were roommates in college, I had a penchant for welcoming each morning by blasting Metallica and eating Cap'n Crunch. Well, Dave resurrected those memories by headbanging into my room, playing "Enter Sandman" on a portable speaker and holding a big box of cereal. Then we watched *Hot Fuzz* on my iPad. Heavy metal, mouth-ripping cereal, and Simon Pegg–good times!

Besides the "escape" and the trip down Memory Lane, Dave and his family have given us love and support of various kinds, and I thank God that we didn't argue too much in college. Eventually I will write about the ultramarathon he and I will conquer. That's right, Dave! It's in print; you have to do it.

People I had never even met assisted us. One of Becky's high school classmates started a GoFundMe account to help us financially, and it raised over $10,000, eventually offsetting the lost wages due to my absence as I quickly ran out of sick days. Law enforcement officers routinely checked on the house; when you live in a small town and flesh-eating bacteria almost kills you, everyone hears about it. That's not to mention the thousands of people who prayed for us in churches across the Midwest. I have reached out to thank as many of those good Samaritans as possible, but I definitely missed some.

Speaking of blessings, the nurses didn't only provide me with world-class professional care. When one stays in the hospital as long as I had, the staff often places a "Getting to know you" poster somewhere in the room. Among the questions asked on my poster was "Favorite movie?" It was 2015, so the Marvel Cinematic

Universe was in its eighth year, and *Avengers: Age of Ultron* actually premiered during my hospital stay (Jeff took me to see it during his second visit from Michigan). While I wasn't the biggest fan of the prequel trilogy, I loved *Star Wars.* I was also a big Monty Python fan, and I owned numerous geeky shirts, so my pick for favorite movie should've been obvious.

Blazing Saddles.

If you aren't familiar, *Blazing Saddles* is a 1974 Western comedy spoof written and directed by Mel Brooks. Not only was the movie released in my birth year and Mel Brooks and I share the same birthdate, *Blazing Saddles* is one of the most daring and hilarious social commentaries ever created. It takes Joseph Campbell's hero's journey archetype, sets it in the Wild West, and injects it with biting social criticism, bawdy humor, sarcastic wit, and one of the best throwaway jokes of all time (you'll need to watch to find it).

I mentioned all that for this moment: One Monday morning, as I lay in my hospital bed and a couple nurses were taking readings, Kris (the head nurse) burst into my room! She practically vibrated with energy for some reason as she started talking.

"HeyChrisIsawthisatagaragesalethisweekendandIthoughtof-yousohereitis!" she sputtered as she thrust something towards me.

I recognized the DVD cover immediately; it was a used copy of *Blazing Saddles.* I stared at it in bewilderment for a moment (I couldn't tell if it were genuine or drug-induced) and then gingerly reached out to grab it from her. I had an exact copy of the movie resting on a shelf back home. However, this one was special, its value instantaneously and exponentially increased by the love and friendship in which it was given. I couldn't believe that Kris gave it to me! I was just a part of her job, an item on her mile-long to-do list. We never even discussed the movie before that morning, yet she paid enough attention to me and my poster that she recognized my favorite movie in a garage sale bin and bought it for me…on her day off, no less!

After my discharge, but before the pandemic, I would run from Bill and Dea's house to the hospital to catch "my" nurses at their 7AM shift change so I could connect with as many of them as possible and let them know how well I was doing and to again thank them for all they had done for me. I also mail them periodic updates, most recently with my professional speaking thank-you card (you know, so I can show them I'm legit).

While I tried to be kind to others in the hospital, I doubled down on learning about everyone I encountered during my hospitalization after receiving Kris' gift. It made my stay friendlier, if not always enjoyable, and to this day I smile when I think about the connections I made.

WHAT'S SO SPECIAL ABOUT GRATITUDE?!

Sometimes I use thankfulness and gratitude interchangeably, but gratitude is actually a more intentional practice. While thankfulness and gratitude can be exercised in basically any situation, gratitude really displays its benefits when times are challenging and even dark.

Author Robert A. Emmons, Ph. D., a current expert and leading researcher in the field of gratitude, has written in his books *Thanks!* and *Gratitude Works!* that "Gratitude has one of the strongest links to mental health and satisfaction with life of any personality trait– more so than even optimism, hope, or compassion." He has then remarked that numerous research studies concluded that gratitude has led to physical, emotional, social, and psychological benefits in virtually every aspect of the human experience[1].

It has not always been a smooth journey to achieve goals after my hospitalization. I have struggled to fulfill my family duties, professional obligations, training schedules, and other facets of my life. Then there's the fact that I look like a Dollar Store zombie when I take off my shirt. Internally, I have contended with constant tightness, discomfort, and pain from those skin grafts. On top of all that, the house and vehicles keep nagging me about "regular maintenance" and "things that need to be fixed." Being grateful for what I have despite those various obstacles has provided me the fortitude to keep focused on the various narrow paths I traverse.

I also realize that, compared to many others, my life is easier/ more blessed/richer (choose your preferred comparative adjective). I know several people who have needed amputations due to NF, who have never secured their preferred occupation, who may not have the family experiences that I have.

Perhaps you are really struggling with one of these issues or something else. If you are, please know that you are why I wrote this book and created this journal. You are in my thoughts, and I am here for you.

You are also not alone. I could list dozens of people who have gone or are going through extremely difficult situations, but someone who has used his own experience to inspire others is Austrian psychiatrist, Holocaust survivor, and author Viktor Frankl. In his book, *Man's Search for Meaning*, Frankl wrote that "Everything can be taken from a man but one thing: the last of the human freedoms—to choose one's attitude in any given set of circumstances, to choose one's own way.[1]"

No matter what you may face or need to overcome, you are free to choose your attitude; remember, where your thoughts go, your mind and body will follow. Whether it's being stuck at a red light or you're on your deathbed, how you view the situation frames the meaning of the event for you. It's a sobering thought that we will all eventually die; how we feel about our circumstances at that time, though, could be the difference between spending our final moments filled with love and gratitude or sadness and regret.

This is not to say that I have enjoyed every experience I've had. In the next section, I'll talk about a few that I'm thankful for because they're over.

MINE EYES DOTH DECEIVE ME!

Something that I didn't enjoy were the hallucinations; I told you I would discuss them. As I mentioned before, Ketamine is a powerful painkiller. It is also an extremely powerful hallucinogenic. I'd never taken powerful drugs before, so hallucinating wasn't something I'd ever experienced. Well, let's just say I made up for lost time.

Right from the time I awoke from my coma, the hallucinations kicked in. I thought I was at the bottom of a water slide, and something like Ecto Cooler was pummeling me. I was actually throwing up CT fluid (I have no idea why I thought it was green). My confusion caused me to yell at the poor nurse who had taken that shift at the last minute…lucky her. My brother was also present for the tirade; he later told me that he also jumped back on the plane and flew home.

The hallucinations held off for several hours until I started imagining that my right pinky had been amputated (remember "robopinky")? I would go back to the traditional classroom setting just so I could point to the whiteboard with my digital digit. (If you've seen my right hand, you'd know that's not the case. Alas.)

The next day, Friday (again, to my immense surprise), offered up more mental hijinks. Becky returned to my hospital room that morning to keep me company. Her presence turned out to be more of a comfort than I could imagine, and I was imagining quite a lot!

A few minutes into her visit, she was chatting with me and holding my hand when I blinked…and the room flipped upside down. I blinked again, and the room stayed upside down. "Whoa!" I exclaimed. "The room's upside down!"

"No, it's not," Becky reassured me as she gently squeezed my hand.

I blinked again. "It's still upside down."

"It's the drugs, dear. It won't last."

Eventually, she was right. But the mind tricks didn't stop there.

A little while later, I saw something move above me. I craned my head upward and set my eyes upon a cloud of tiny bugs hovering around an open window. "Eww, the window's open, and there are bugs!"

Becky released a moderately sized sigh and said, "The window's not open."

"I see bugs! AND the window's open!"

(Another sigh) "We are in an ICU room in the Mayo Clinic, and it's March. The window. Is. Not. Open."

"OK." I was still skeptical.

A few moments after that, I noticed another annoyance, but this one was harder to shake. I started hearing music, but it wasn't just any song.

It was "The Macarena."

"Can someone please shut off the music?"

"What music?"

"The radio keeps playing 'The Macarena.'"

(Another big sigh) "There isn't a radio in the ICU, sweetie."

An hour after that, I saw a giant.

Actually, it was my brother John visiting from South St. Paul. He's 6'6".

As I had experienced numerous extensive surgeries, I remained dependent on Ketamine for several weeks while I recovered. This meant I hallucinated…a lot. Even in my sleep. One vivid dream involved a Bavarian Forest with rolling hills just outside my hospital room, and occasionally a team of 20 male Eastern European gymnasts would tumble their way over the landscape, executing acrobatic rolls and flips over logs and rocks. It was quite impressive!

I also remembered the trip from my ICU room to Francis 2C, the wing and floor where I spent the vast majority of my hospitalization. The darkened hallways engulfed us as the nurses and other staff wheeled me to Room 111. As they turned me into the doorway, I glanced to the right; I could have sworn I saw a giant hydraulic piston. What was THAT doing there?!

I was also ABSOLUTELY certain that I had brought my travel bag with me. Despite Becky assuring me that I had not, I kept asking for it. Then there's the sack of comics (complete with a Tesseract hologram projector that showed scenes from the MCU movies) that I swore I saw in the next room, which turned out to be my bathroom.

While I didn't appreciate the side effects of Ketamine, I am grateful that it lessened the pain I felt during much of my hospitalization. It also strengthened my resolve to cease my reliance on my medications as soon as possible.

However, that's a lesson that I would fully learn at another time.

BREATHE...

As my recovery progressed, I began more physical treatments. First, I lost the catheter. Perhaps it was another effect of the drugs that I didn't realize that I had one to lose.

Then I began hyperbaric oxygen treatments. If you're not familiar, a hyperbaric oxygen treatment consists of breathing pure oxygen in a sealed room for numerous sessions. My experience differs from others since the Mayo Clinic's facilities are unique. They were housed on the first floor of Methodist Hospital, which was a few blocks from St. Mary's. So, for each of the 15 oxygen treatment sessions, ambulance drivers fetched me from my room, wheeled me to the hospital garage, drove me to Methodist, unloaded me, and pushed me into the front door of the hospital. From there they turned me to the right and entered through the treatment facility doors. Once I gave a staff member my name and patient number, they issued me a waiting room until the current treatment session ended.

Once my session was ready, they wheeled me into the oxygen chamber; in later sessions, I just walked. The chamber was sectioned into two areas with a bathroom in the center. Each area contained five or six leather recliners that faced a flat-screen TV. I usually sat in the back; I didn't watch TV. I usually ordered cranberry juice to sip as the staff prepped the room. I made sure to finish my drink before the session started; I couldn't drink it during the session.

To ensure that patients received as much pure oxygen as possible, we had to wear transparent, plastic, cylindrical helmets that had tubes running to oxygen tanks. If you recall Mr. Freeze from the fantastic *Batman: The Animated Series*, imagine a cheap knock-off cosplay version of his helmet. Once we donned the helmets and were ready to start, the VERY large doors closed, and the session started.

Each session was divided into two 45-minutes segments, with a five-minute break. Of the 15 sessions I enjoyed, I only stayed awake for one of those sessions, and it wasn't for the entire time. I experienced some of the best naps throughout my hospitalization in those oxygen treatment sessions!

...AND STRETCH!

During the time span in which I partook in the oxygen treatments, I also started my physical and occupational therapies. During my first conversation with Tanya, my physical therapist, I told her what I wanted to do, which is to get back to my previous physical ability level. She commended me for my fortitude, but she also stated that it would not be easy considering how much my body endured to survive.

The first trial I remember undertaking was walking from my room to the nearest nurse's station, which was directly across the hall. As I mentioned before, a week before my hospitalization, I had run a Pi Day race (3.14 miles) in 19:29. I prided myself on being in the top 10% of any race field. A 30-foot round trip shouldn't have even been an afterthought; now, it was brutal! By the time I parked my walker next to my bed and collapsed, I was physically wiped out; surprisingly, though, I was not mentally beaten. Sure, my ego took a hit, but what should I have expected? I had been bedridden for three weeks, I was missing body parts, and the muscles I still had were atrophied. At the very least, I knew one thing; I would only get stronger.

Sure enough, I soon found myself walking to the next nurses' station (another 40 feet away) and the one after that, about another 50 feet away. Concurrently, I started using a portable pulley system that I attached to the bathroom door. I would gingerly lower myself to the floor, scooch my butt to the door, grab the handles, and lower one straightened arm while raising the other. My right arm, free of the yellow cocoon, was comically skinny. Further, it couldn't straighten as far as my left due to the skin grafts, but I gritted my teeth and pushed against the grafts for every millimeter I could get. I also squeezed a set of three sponges that Tanya gave me to strengthen my right hand. The #1 sponge (creatively named that because it had a 1 on it) was easy to crush; #3 was considerably denser and took much more effort to collapse. Additionally, she gifted me a green plastic "tennis racquet" and a yellow "tennis ball"; the quotation marks mean that they weren't really those items…you get it. Tanya challenged me to first bounce the fake tennis ball on the fake tennis racquet a few times; when I mastered that, she tasked me to bounce the ball 20 consecutive times. Once bouncing was no longer a challenge, she told me to flip the racquet from one side to the other mid-bounce; this proved a bit more challenging. My wrist and forearm were tight from the surgeries, so a complete 180° turn did not come naturally.

Over time, my dexterity and strength increased. The walks to the nurses' station with a walker evolved into walks to different sections of the hospital with first a cane, then nothing. The shoulder exercises became easier, as did the sponge squeezes (even #3).

The tennis racquet exercises also increased my wrist and forearm strength, so much so that I developed more definition in my thand, the flap of skin doctors took from my thigh. I was told that flaps (like my thand) rarely settled down, and yet mine was almost flush with my original hand skin. That happened because I kept working on my exercises, no matter how painful they felt or how boring they were.

One of the indicators that I was well on my way to "total" physical recovery came from a moment of forgetfulness. After one of my final sessions with Tanya, I remembered that I had to tell her something. Without thinking about it, I bolted out of my hospital room, darted to the stairwell door, and bounded up a few steps to give her the message. After giving her the message, I walked back to my room and encountered a couple nurses who apparently were not expecting me to do that. Apparently, they don't often have patients sprinting through the hallway. I was winded as I returned to my bed, but I was more excited that I was capable of such speed.

Besides participating in physical therapy, I also worked on my nutrition (OK, aside from the pizza). One task I was given was the consumption of protein shakes. As an athlete, I have developed an affinity for protein shakes. That said, I usually only consumed one a day.

The nutritionist tasked me with drinking three shakes daily.

If I were training for a long-distance race like a half or full marathon, three protein shakes a day would NOT be a problem. My daily mileage would require me to consume thousands of calories. In the hospital, I barely walked 1,000 steps a day. I hadn't done a single push-up, pullup, or squat. The workouts I was doing barely qualified as glorified stretching. So, drinking/eating three extremely thick protein shakes became workouts in themselves. I literally needed to breathe through bites on occasion, as if I were a competitive eater trying to scarf down that 50th hot dog.

That said, I discovered motivation in eating those cement-like shakes in a single number: 70. The nutritionist placed 70kg (about 154 lbs.) as a benchmark for me to reach; I weighed in around 58kg at this time. I'd hovered between 70.4kg and 72.7kg (155 and 160 lbs.), respectively, throughout the majority of my adult life before my hospitalization, so 70 shouldn't be an issue…

…right?!

I was never more frustrated in the hospital than when I stepped on the scale and saw numbers like 62.5 and 65 pop up. It truly stumped me how I could not reach 70. As it turns out, your body burns A LOT of calories when it's healing itself. I must've ordered the pizza at least three days in a row multiple days at a time so I could gain that weight.

Finally, I had gained enough weight and healed enough that doctors decided that I could be discharged on Tuesday, May 26th. Coincidentally, Jeff, his Becky, and their daughter Hope drove over from Michigan to see us for the Memorial Day weekend. They stayed at a Rochester hotel, and I spent most of their stay outside the hospital. They all went swimming at the hotel pool, which was fun for them; I had to stay out of the water because the wounds on my back hadn't completely healed.

When I returned to the hospital, the nursing staff offered me some interesting information: I had been moved to a different room on the same floor. I felt disappointed that I couldn't finish my stay in the room where I spent the most time, but given what all I had experienced, it was a tiny thing to lament.

I was free (or so I thought)…

During the last few days of my hospitalization, I stopped taking the rest of my medications (notably oxycontin and oxycodone). I was determined to avoid addiction at all costs thanks to my Ketamine experience, and it was going well.

Was.

I was scheduled to leave the hospital on May 26th at 10:00AM.

Bill arrived at the hospital around 8:30AM to help me pack up my belongings. When he came into my room, I was putting stuff into a receptacle, but it wasn't what he had in mind.

I was throwing up...from drinking orange juice.

Withdrawal had set in. The irony was not lost on me even as I shook at the side of my hospital bed. I would vomit two more times before FINALLY being discharged at 6:30PM. After two months of hospitalization, hard work, and solid progress, my struggle to actually LEAVE the facility screamed anticlimactic. I eventually sat in a wheelchair for the final time and sprang out of it to strike a sprinter's pose just outside the hospital doors...twice; I didn't pose correctly the first time.

Throughout that entire day, Bill never showed frustration. He was the picture of patience, rolling with each change of plans. He allowed me to curse myself for going cold turkey but never said so much as a "told you so." That day was a snapshot into what makes Bill a great man and dad.

HOME THERAPY

After my hospitalization, Dr. Bakri recommended that I participate in three weeks of home therapy so nurses could dress the open wounds on my back and continue my physical therapy. I spent the first 10 days at Bill and Dea's house in Rochester. Bill drove me back to New Ulm where I finished the remainder of home therapy. When I was staying at Bill and Dea's, I really enjoyed spending more time with them. Bill stopped by my hospital room numerous times throughout my hospitalization in both professional and personal capacities, and Dea had made frequent visits to play a Scrabble-type game on my iPad. That said, though, I relished the opportunity to interact with them without having IVs attached to me or nurses taking readings constantly. I watched more *Big Bang Theory* in those 10 days than I had in my entire life. I hadn't been actively avoiding it before, but as a geek myself, it almost felt like watching an alternate version of my own life.

Something I COULD do in Rochester that I discovered I couldn't do in New Ulm during home therapy was walk outside. New Ulm is a much smaller community than Rochester, and many people knew my situation. If someone from the hospital saw me or knew I was walking around town, my home therapy might be terminated; I still needed it because I still had open wounds that required dressing, and I needed a physical therapist to observe that I had reached an adequate level of self-sufficiency with my exercises. The alley behind our house beckoned to me, inviting me to slip on my running shoes and experience that little slice of heaven once again. However, I successfully resisted the urge to exercise outside and only ventured out to church (which was allowed).

Despite my slight disappointment, my first post-discharge appointment proved to be a mental game changer. Becky drove us back to Rochester for a couple days and a check-up with Dr. Bakri. During our appointment, I asked him about my restrictions with my "new" body. Dr Bakri wryly answered, "Chris, you are the first marathon runner that I know of who's contracted NF, so you tell us."

Boom!

I felt a door unlock inside my mind. I now had license to explore the upper limits of my physical abilities, something I actually didn't fully consider. Sure, I had bought new running shoes while I was in the hospital, but I realized that was an act of wishful thinking. With Dr. Bakri's words, my wishes could now become actions.

ON THE ROAD AGAIN

A COUPLE DAYS AFTER THAT appointment, I received my final day of home therapy. After that, I would still receive outpatient physical therapy, but I could finally go places, I could be seen by others…I could run! So, the nurse dressed my wounds (which were mostly healed; Becky could do the rest) and handed me the service termination papers. I signed them slightly hastily and watched her back out of the driveway. As soon as she traveled down the alley, I grabbed those aforementioned shoes and quickly started to run down the road. A friend of mine had experienced her own health issue during my hospitalization, so I headed to the office where she worked. It was about a kilometer away, so I didn't think too much about the distance. I made it to her office feeling pretty good: A bit winded, but otherwise fine. We chatted for a few minutes, and then I ventured back home. The second part of my run informed me of an EXTREMELY important fact: I had not run in three months!

When my running watch chimed at the one-mile mark, I stumbled to a halt, thrust my hands behind my thrown back head and screamed! (I'll leave what I screamed to your imagination.) Everything BURNED! My legs, my lungs, my right arm…they were all on fire! Frustration crept inside of me; how much have I regressed?!? Apparently, that much.

As I shuffled back home (which was about a block away), those burning sensations slowly ebbed. That flicker of hope Dr. Bakri ignited on our post-discharge appointment caught the tapestry of

my ambitions, setting them aflame. I can run again! Yes, that first mile was terrible, but I can improve. So, the next day, I planned to "run" two miles; it was actually glorified walking. However, I wisely alternated between running and walking each block. I certainly felt better than the day before; breathing did not hurt nearly as badly, and the soreness in my legs didn't increase as I thought it would. A few days later, I ran two blocks and walked one. A few after that, I stretched the run to three blocks. A month after being discharged from home therapy, I ran/walked a local 5K with Josh, then six years old. It felt great to travel that distance on my own, especially when I would think back three months when I could barely make it across the hospital hallway using a walker.

I should state that, while I have accomplished a number of

running personal milestones, I do need to deal with issues most runners rarely (if ever) consider. First of all, since my left leg is missing a considerably large muscle, my left leg would fatigue more quickly than my right one when I go for long runs in the first few years post-surgery. Thankfully, the other muscles have wonderfully compensated. The much larger issue I deal with on a daily basis is the great size of the skin graft area that encompasses the upper right side of my body. Skin grafts are nonporous, which means that they don't sweat. Heat cannot escape through my skin like it can throughout the rest of my body, thereby limiting homeostasis (the body's ability to regulate its own internal temperature). As I type these words, my right arm is extremely warm and tight. I need to constantly stretch my arm and shoulder so that the skin grafts don't constrict worse, and I lose any more range of motion. As it is, due to the area connecting my right pectoral to my shoulder, my volleyball block is horribly subpar, and I look like a parenthesis when I do a pull-up because of the skin grafts' constriction. (see the pull-up picture).

To gain an understanding of what I experience, take some cellophane or similar plastic material, and wrap it around your arm over and over. Tighten the material until it feels like someone is giving you a snakebite; that's what I feel on my right side ALL THE TIME. I moisturize the area often so it feels cooler and doesn't dry out.

Having that latest race under my belt, I felt emboldened to enter more events within the following months, such as a trail 5K in Michigan, another 5K in New Ulm supporting the public school system, and a 10K in a nearby town (where I even finished 2nd in my division). In later years, I have set/tied four lifetime personal running records in the 5K (tie), 10K, 10-mile, and half marathon. Eventually, I set my heights higher (longer, actually), but there was another milestone I decided to pursue first, all thanks to my older son.

EVERYBODY WAS TAE KWON DO FIGHTING!

My older son Josh started Tae Kwon Do (TKD) in Fall 2015 when he started 1st grade. I had also studied TKD as a middle schooler, but I quit before earning my Black Belt because I entered high school and "got stupid" (my words entirely). As I aged and thought about what I would like to do in my life, securing my Black Belt occasionally popped up. Throughout that first year of his TKD studies, I attended his weekly classes and realized that I wanted to participate in them as much as he did. I even joined some of the classes out of boredom, which was my sneaky way to tip my toe in the water and see if I wanted to retry TKD. "Mortality motivation" also influenced my desire to join. Mortality motivation is the concept that you are acutely aware that life is finite, so you are more driven to accomplish more with your remaining time. Being so close to losing my life definitely enlightened me to that fact.

Once Josh had made it a year and earned his Green Belt, I asked him if I could join him in his classes. Thankfully, he said, "Yes." There was someone else I needed to approach before I could begin my studies: Master Esmaeil Torabpour. Master Torabpour was a middle-aged Middle Eastern man about an inch shorter than I with extremely short salt-and-pepper hair. I approached him and described my history with TKD, where I earned my Brown Belt before quitting, and my desire to join Josh as a Green Belt, and Master Torabpour agreed. So, I gave him a check for my first year of training, and he gave me a white uniform and a Green Belt.

It felt good to wear a TKD uniform again. I quickly caught up to where Josh was not only with the moves, but also with the required level of physicality. I had taken up boxing in college and, while I had all of one fight under my belt, I sparred a great deal. One of the very first lessons I learned in my pugilistic studies was how to establish a solid stance and foundation; in fact, my first two weeks focused solely on my stance with my trainer walking around, pushing me to test my balance. I discovered that those weeks of stance training had become second nature as I restarted my TKD classes. I stepped into sparring sessions with more confidence and, admittedly, some pent-up aggression. I didn't seriously hurt anyone, but let's just say I needed to rein myself in during a couple bouts in the beginning. I have to say, though, physically besting people half to a third of your age is a nice boost for your ego.

In our quest for our Black Belts, Josh and I had to attend martial arts tournaments hosted by Master Torabpour; some of them were intraschool tournaments where students from Master Torabpour's other schools attended (he had four other locations besides New Ulm), and others featured schools from other disciplines. However, they all took place in St. Mary's School in Owatonna, MN, about a mile from Master Torabpour's flagship school. Josh and I always did reasonably well at those tournaments. While every participant left with (at least) a 3rd place trophy or medal for each event they entered, we frequently brought home 1st or 2nd place hardware. I won most often for form and sparring; the only time I didn't place 1st for sparring was two weeks after running a half marathon PR of 1:29:13 which took place three weeks after running a Ragnar Ultra (I'll explain later) where I ran 33.5 miles within a span of 24 hours at an average pace of 7:45. Suffice it to say, I was NOT as limber at that tournament as I usually was.

Not that I was incredibly flexible in the first place. When you are a long-distance runner in your 40s, your hip flexors aren't very flexy. Perhaps the most difficult part of my TKD training was increasing my flexibility as I continued to run constantly. The running gave me a pronounced endurance edge in the ring, but it held my more difficult kicks back (or, rather, down). Two of the requirements for the Black Belt were slow-motion kicks, a front kick and a roundhouse kick, both for each leg. Every part of each maneuver had to be performed at a snail's pace with no falter in form. I had decent balance for the most part, but my constantly tight hip flexors and hamstrings hampered me from fully extending my legs past my waist. I would raise my knee past my belt, but as I extended my foot away from my body, my leg would slowly drop, often ending with my foot lower than my solar plexus, my target height. Thankfully, I was allowed to start my kick with the kicking leg in front, so I had less work to do.

When completing the requirements for my Black Belt, I completed the front kicks somewhat easily; the roundhouse kicks proved more troublesome. In fact, the right roundhouse kick was the very last requirement I passed. To clarify, the process to earn a Black Belt included two separate tests. After each test, I received a sheet that included portions of the test I passed, and those on which I needed to improve. I performed better on my second test than my first, but I still had some portions that I needed to improve, including (no surprise to me) slow-motion roundhouse kicks. So, a month and a half after the second test, I ran to the New Ulm school at 6:00 AM on a late December morning, unlocked the door, and recorded myself successfully performing the slow-motion roundhouse kick on my right leg.

Now that I have reached this long-term goal, I have turned my focus to other endeavors. I might eventually continue my TKD training, but I will never forget the lessons of perseverance and patience I have learned in this chapter of my life, nor the people who've helped me along the way.

One more thing about TKD: While I could perform every task asked of me, Becky did place one restriction on me. Since so much money, time, and attention was given to my right arm, she told me that I could not perform breaks with it. However, she enacted this restriction AFTER I fractured a knuckle when I errantly broke two boards at once; I was in a board-breaking competition and rashly added a board to one of the breaks in a combo I created. (Note: I did NOT win. Lesson painfully learned.)

AIMING FOR BOSTON

DESPITE MY SUCCESSES IN THE shorter running distances, the marathon was a thorn in my ego. I'd never had good marathon experiences due to inadequate training and injuries due to inadequate training. However, I always felt a tinge of jealousy whenever I saw someone wearing Boston Marathon merchandise. While it may seem cliché to say that you "want to run Boston," I still wanted to earn that yellow jacket and demonstrate that those who've survived a traumatic life event (like surviving NF) can achieve great physical feats. I could probably raise enough money to run Boston, but I wanted to earn my way to the starting line by running a qualifying time (which, thank goodness, lowers every five years).

Just as one does not simply walk into Mordor, one does not simply run a BQ. To make my marathon venture more successful, I hired a coach named Andrew Snow who specializes in helping people qualify for Boston. I had been following him on Facebook and YouTube for around a year and even interacted with him briefly, but I never officially worked with him. After attending his Boston Academy webinar in early December 2022, though, I realized that I needed to take action on that marathon goal, and Andrew would help me with that.

I first looked up the time I needed to run to qualify for Boston. According to baa.org, I needed to run a marathon under three hours and 20 minutes, as that was the designated qualifying time for male runners aged 45-49 (I would be 49 on race day). This would be over 25 minutes faster than my current marathon PR: A substantial time difference, but certainly not improbable.

The next step to achieving my goal was to pick a marathon to run (a trivial matter, I know). Andrew stated in the webinar that a training cycle should last at least 16 weeks, or about four months, but it could last 20 weeks or more. I jumped onto a Minnesota racing site and searched for Spring 2023 Boston Marathon-qualifying marathons, and one particular race caught my eye: The Med City Marathon in Rochester, MN.

As someone who really appreciates a well-played full circle moment, I immediately looked up the race details for Med City. It would run on Saturday, May 13, 2023, so that would give me 20 weeks of training. It was 26.68 miles long, so almost a half mile longer than the traditional marathon distance. This longer distance is actually normal for Boston qualifying marathons; race directors want to make sure their participants have the best shot to qualify on their course, as running a course shorter than 26.2 miles would not be considered for Boston.

What caught my attention the most was the elevation map. The race started by the Rochester International Airport and traveled for about six miles on rolling hills before descending about 200 feet over the course of two miles before entering Rochester proper. From there it ran an uneven perimeter around the city until it finally finished right in front of the Mayo Civic Center. Until mile 20 the course kept up the rolling hills motif that the first six miles started. Mile 20, though, introduced the first of three deceptive hills.

Once I started working with him as a student, I realized why my previous 26.2-mile attempts had concluded in such frustrating fashions: I was running too fast in my training.

Yes, that's right! I had run my training runs too fast, which taxed my body so much that it broke down during the race. Andrew illuminated the notion of running my easy miles slowly, or in his words, "embarrassingly slow," like 9:00 and 10:00/mile paces. (Note: "Slowly" is truly subjective here, and I do not look down upon anyone's running speed. I respect all runners, no matter their running speeds). In my particular case, though, as someone who used to pride himself on running normal runs at a 7:30/mile pace, it was eye-opening to consider running slowly to get faster.

However, when I ran more slowly, I could accrue more mileage with less injury risk. That doesn't mean I DIDN'T get injured during my marathon training, but I bounced back from those physical hiccups more quickly. I also incorporated regular strength training sessions into my weeks, which forced me to strengthen muscle groups that are typically ignored by regular running, such as the glute muscles (which, let me tell you, can be a real pain in the butt if you neglect them).

Additionally, I worked harder on sleeping at least 7 ½ to 8 hours each night. As an early morning runner, that meant I had to stop working on my various projects earlier, especially if I wanted to have some time with Becky after the kids were in bed.

I used to worry about not getting enough done in the day, so that would mean I would work well into the night. Marathon training, if nothing else, demands that you develop and maintain solid time management skills, so I made a conscious choice to "do all I could do" each day. Once I did that, I put everything down and prepared for bed.

My training started on Friday, December 8th, 2022. Before I started training, I was logging about 35 miles a week. That amount floated around that number for the first couple months; sustaining a minor knee injury in early January 2023 certainly dropped that average down. Going into February, I launched into the 40 miles/week average territory for the first time in the training, and that amount only dropped once (38.9 miles) before May 13th.

Running slowly for at least 80% of the time not only kept me from sustaining more injuries, my body also became increasingly stronger. Mind you, I wasn't bench pressing 600 lbs., but I handled my increased mileage better than I have in previous marathon attempts. Additionally, I incorporated more strength training into my regimen, adding the use of a kettlebell. I'd never used a kettlebell before, so my lateral muscles initially questioned this life choice; consistency eventually won out, however, and my entire body has benefited ever since.

NUTRITION

It is often said that abs are made in the kitchen. Scientifically speaking, this saying is inaccurate and extremely unsanitary. Figuratively speaking, it is true. No matter how hard you work out, you can't make significant athletic progress if you eat fast food and processed foods all day.

Contrary to popular belief, running does NOT offer you a free pass to eat whatever you want. I started eating more greens and fruits on a daily basis, including making myself spinach salads and fruit smoothies every day. This also meant switching my breakfast protein shake formula from whey protein to plant-based protein. As a result, my body didn't have to work out those "problematic" additives and other junk as much, and my internal systems operated more efficiently.

Pro-tip: Think of baby oranges as extra-juicy fruit snacks.

THE RUNS...NOT THOSE RUNS!

It goes without saying that you need to run a lot to properly train for a marathon. However, it must be said that you need to run strategically to get the most out of your time on the road, track, trail, or treadmill. This is where Andrew's training really kicked in for me.

Earlier I mentioned that at least 80% of my miles were slow. That leaves about 20% for other speeds. In the first third of my training cycle, I ran eight to 10 100-meter strides almost every workout. Strides are short bursts of speed where you run comfortably fast; I would pump my arms faster to increase my cadence to a fast but relaxed speed for a few seconds and then slow down gradually. I also ran 8-second hill sprints through my easy runs, where I would pick a hill and go out for eight seconds. Then I would keep running easy until my heart rate settled down, at which time I would find another hill and sprint again. Between the slow miles, strides, and hill sprints, my weekly mileage averaged in the high 30s, aside from the weeks I had to cross train due to a small injury.

For the second third of my training, I incorporated more specific speed workouts. Once a week I ran shorter intervals that were much faster than my goal marathon race pace, as well as a longer workout that was significantly slower than that goal marathon race pace (but not "easy" pace). I still worked in the strides and hill sprints, which meant my weekly mileage increased in this section of training from the high 30s to the mid-to-high 40s.

For the final third of my training, I incorporated even more specific speed workouts. Those faster intervals lengthened in distance but slowed to be a few seconds faster than my goal marathon race pace. The other workout acted as a true tempo run (think "comfortably hard") that was slightly slower than that goal marathon race pace. By this section, my weekly mileage increased again, many weeks climbing into the 50s; a couple weeks even reached the 60-mile mark.

One crucial part of my training was the implementation of long runs. Long runs, more than any other kind of workout, provided me with the most realistic marathon practice I could ask for. Obviously, they challenged me to run multiple miles at one time, but they also put my mental strength through the figurative paces[1].

As I trained mostly by myself, no one else was watching and nagging me to run faster or not give up. I could have easily walked those miles or even just slept in.

However, **I** would have known.

I ran the vast majority of the long runs on Saturdays (the one exception being the Sunday I ran the Goldy's 10 Mile in Minneapolis–more on that later). Starting in late January, my first long run was 11 miles. For the most part, I increased the distance of each long run by about a mile. As the race date approached, I combined my long run and my tempo (comfortably hard) run on many Saturdays; I would start the run slow, complete the tempo part of the run, and then finish slow (which, let me tell you, was NOT a problem).

Along with the extra miles, I also practiced taking nutrition on the long runs. This consisted of packing 40g gels in my pockets and a fuel belt holding two small bottles: one half full of water, and the other half full of electrolyte fuel. I would take one gel after two miles (or 20 minutes) and then one every three miles, followed by some water. For the most part, the fueling worked well for the first four gels, but it would be a struggle to finish the others. Towards the end of training, I chalked up that struggle to just getting used to taking in nutrition in the later stages of the long run.

The longest long run I completed was 22.02 miles, which I ran in three hours and 41 seconds. It was a mostly flat and straight out-and-back route from New Ulm to the outskirts of Sleepy Eye (yes, like from *Little House on the Prairie*). The first 11 miles were run at around an 8:45/mile pace, with the next eight miles ranging from 7:24 to 7:38. Other than the fantastic workout it offered, that run reinforced a classic tactic of using an out-and-back route: Check which direction the wind is blowing BEFORE you head out.

GOLDY'S RUN

About six weeks before the marathon, I ran the Goldy's 10 Mile race with my friend Mike Benz. The race started on the University of Minnesota campus just outside Huntington Bank Stadium, ran alongside the Mississippi River, and finished on the 50-yard line of the football field. We signed up for Goldy's before I decided to run Med City, but it actually served as a good barometer for how well my training was progressing. Despite the unpleasant cold snap and intermittent freezing drizzle, I sustained a strong pace (7:00 min/pace) throughout the first half and incrementally picked up the pace until the ninth mile when I encountered about an entire mile of hills. The 10th mile did prove that my training had made a difference, though, as I energetically pumped my arms as I rounded the final corner, entered the Huntington Bank Stadium tunnel, and sprinted to the 50-yard finish line.

I crossed the line in 1:09:12, averaging about 6:56/mile. If I multiplied that average by 26.2, that would hypothetically give me a marathon time of 3:01:18, which would definitely put me under the age division cap of 3:20. That didn't really matter, though; running 10 miles is NOT running 26.2, and a lot can happen in those extra 16+ miles. All in all, Goldy's provided me with a solid idea of where I was physically; I was headed in the right direction, but I still needed to stay focused on the training regimen.

Finally, the week preceding the race arrived. A few weeks prior, I had experienced a case of "maranoia," an anecdotal phenomenon where one becomes a mental landscape artist by creating mountains out of molehills. Every little twinge or momentary pain sent me into a potential panic!

"Ooh, my calf feels tight; I better call Dr. Fred (my chiropractor)."

"Uh, my quad is a little sore. Give me the ibuprofen. No, ALL of the ibuprofen!"

"Ah! I grazed my toe on that step! Do you think they'll reschedule the race if I asked really nicely?!"

"Achoo! Call a priest to administer last rites! I know I'm not Catholic; JUST DO IT!!!"

Thankfully, all of those "potentially disastrous" ailments subsided, and I found a greater sense of inner peace before the week of May 8th.

I did have one question for Andrew as the week began. I usually didn't eat before my runs, and he had said in a couple training videos to take in some calories a few hours before the race. As I try to adhere to the principle of "NEVER do anything new on race day," I messaged him to ask what I should do. He suggested that I practice having something in my stomach as I ran each day that week so I know what it felt like on race day.

So, I bought an inexpensive juicer and a big bag of oranges. Each night, I juice three oranges and put the cup in the fridge. In the morning, the very first (or second) thing I did after waking up was down that cup of OJ. All in all, I couldn't tell the difference in having the juice in my system, so I counted that as a good thing.

As per Andrew's coaching, I also didn't taper (drop my mileage drastically) that week. Since the vast majority of my miles were run at an easy pace, I wasn't exhausting my body during my daily workouts. I cut off a mile or so off each one and just woke up a little bit later, trying to get as much rest as I could.

RACE DAY (ALMOST)!

As I stated earlier, one of the reasons I asked to be sent to Mayo was because Bill and Dea lived in Rochester. This came in clutch for the marathon because not only did they live in Rochester, they lived on the race course (but more on that later). They also lived less than two miles from the race expo/finish line. So, the day before the race, Becky and I packed up the kids after school and drove to Rochester. We arrived at their house, and while Becky and the kids visited with Bill and Dea, I picked up my race bib and shirt at the expo. I also confirmed where the buses would be to shuttle runners to the start line.

We ate dinner (spaghetti with garlic bread and salad) and just lounged about while I laid out my running gear. I then went to bed around 8:30 PM. Becky and I have a tradition of playing 500, a popular Midwestern card game, with Bill and Dea after the kids go to bed, but this was a special occasion, so we decided to save the game for another day.

RACE DAY (ACTUALLY)!

I woke up at 4:40 AM on race day. Since the race started at 7:00 AM, I wanted to give myself enough time to get ready, take the shuttle to the start line, and warm up without feeling pressed for time. Becky was kind enough to drop me off at the shuttle bus pickup at 5:30. From there, I hopped onto the bus, chatted with some fellow runners on the way to the airport, and arrived at the start line. I rocked out a two-mile warmup, went to the restroom, found my friend Blake, a former New Ulm Run Club runner and Ragnar teammate, and then entered the bag dropoff line. Despite the dropoff line being WAY too long and the need to use the bathroom reemerging, I arrived at the start line and reunited with Blake a couple minutes before the race started. The race director thanked us for running our respective races (a half marathon and 20-mile race were also happening), the National Anthem played over the sound system, and then we were off.

Blake and I ran together for the first 4.5 miles, logging about 7:20/mile. This worked perfectly into my overall running plan, as I would run the first 8.5 miles around that pace, speed up to 7:10/mile until mile 21, and then gut it out for the last 5+ miles. He needed to make a pit stop at mile 4.5, so he wished me well, and I kept on going.

The rest of the first 8.5 miles went as planned. I saw a teaching colleague at mile 6 (thanks for the support, Kelsy!) and picked up the pace a tad when I hit two miles of descent. I didn't speed up too much, as running hard downhill would wear out my quads and make the last part of the race torturous. As I entered the Rochester city limits, I also entered the second phase of my plan and sped up to about 7:10/mile.

Those first 4.5 miles were uneventful, other than the slight elevation fluctuation. I rose from a riverside bike path around the halfway mark and felt my speed slow a bit. However, I took a few deep breaths, focused on my arm swing, and caught back up to my pace. Easy peasy!

Just before mile 15, Becky, Bill, Dea, and the kids met me on the corner right outside Bill and Dea's cul-de-sac, and I exchanged my fuel belt for a running bottle and shedded my shirt. Something I didn't account for during my training was that I layered up more during those long runs, so the fuel belt was actually looser and bounced around more during the race. This caused some chafing on my back, so losing the belt was actually more beneficial than I anticipated. Seeing my family more than halfway through the marathon was the best benefit, though! I instinctively picked up my race a little too much, so I needed to rein in the speed a bit as we parted ways. The next five miles were quite enjoyable; even veering off the bike path to avoid an entire family of geese put a smile on my face.

Then I found myself at a crossroads…literally.

As my watch registered 20 miles, I approached a T intersection. I saw people going both ways, so I asked the volunteers which way I should go. They were in the midst of a conversation and didn't initially see me, which led to some immediate confusion. One of them said "Right," so I started heading that way. Then I heard the utterance "Sorry, I mean left" and started saying bad words in my head. I don't begrudge the volunteers for not seeing me; it wasn't like I was screaming my approach from 100 feet away that I was coming, and volunteering at a race can sometimes be long and boring.

That minor event did mark a downhill turn in my speed, however. For the first time in the race, I felt sluggish and tired. I also knew I was about to run…er, shuffle up three hills, so the race had turned into a true battle of wills. At the 20-mile mark, I had been running for 2 hours and 24 minutes, averaging a 7:14/mile pace. I also had followed my nutrition intake regimen by ingesting a gel packet every about three miles. Apparently, my body still wasn't cool with that because I could feel my stomach working…never a good sign during a marathon. So, between my speed and my stomach, my body and my mind were ready to rumble.

That first hill wasn't that high, about 60 feet over the course of a quarter mile. In my current condition, it could've been 60 inches, and I still would've struggled. Every step felt heavier than the last, so I started using 2nd-person self-talk, things like "You can do it, Chris," "Let's go, Chris," "You got this," and "Shut up, legs!" Gravity patiently waited for me on the top of the hill and helped me make up some lost time. Gravity wasn't the only one waiting for me, though.

Blake's wife Andrea (a phenomenal warrior in her own right) and their two kids, Dayson and Sarah, were camped out at the bottom of the hill. As I approached them, Andrea hollered encouragements at me and took one of my favorite pictures of me running. I made a point of smiling at least once during every mile of the race, and she caught me at just the right time.

After seeing Andrea and the kids, I picked up the pace slightly and started doing mental math to calculate the pace I needed to keep so I could break 3:20. This helped me pass the time without dwelling too much on my struggle.

That worked for about two miles.

As I entered mile 23, I put my mental calculator through the ringer. With each glance at my watch to check my current pace, I worked out what speed I needed to cross the finish line under my goal time. With each calculation, the realization that I may not achieve my goal started to gain traction in my mind. Five months of training, dozens of pre-dawn runs in freezing weather, hundreds of dollars spent in gear and tutelage…all wasted in the course of six miles.

I even considered the thought of slowing to a walk to quell some of the pain I was feeling. If my feet could talk, they would not be allowed around pleasant company; an R rating would not be out of the question. Someone also replaced my calf muscles with rocks, which was rude!

I thought of everyone who had supported me in this endeavor, and how they would react to my "failure." They would be disappointed for me, but not in me. Most of them had never run a marathon and would still be proud of me for trying, and those who had run the distance knew that anything can happen between the start line and the finish. They would be OK with the result.

But I wouldn't be.

Like I did in that hospital room a few miles away but eight years prior, I told myself that I would not "waste" their faith in me. I wouldn't let this challenge hold me down or keep me back. I would rise up and conquer this!

So, after a quick prayer and a deep breath, I pumped my arms a little faster and focused not on the finish line, but on the turn in front of me. Once I reached that turn, I turned my attention to the next one, and the next, and the next. I also caught up to slower 20-

mile runners, grunting encouragement to each of them as I passed. Pretty soon, I reached the bridge that ran under Broadway St, and it was time to play the song.

"HOLDIN' OUT..."

Early in my marathon training, I started listening to music on my runs. Over my years of running, I'd gone back and forth between listening to music/podcasts and running "soundless". I knew that to train properly, I had to run for hours at a time, and I could not afford to hire race spectators to shout at me on Saturday mornings in February and March (not that they would want to, especially in Minnesota). So, I adopted an earlier playlist for Med City.

Most of the songs on my playlist fell into the hard rock/heavy metal category. Some of the songs included "Master of Puppets" by Metallica, Survivor's "Eye of the Tiger," and the fast version of Queen's "We Will Rock You." (Yes, there's a fast version, and it blows the original out of the water!) I also employed some songs by Linkin Park, and I even tossed in a couple tracks from *Hamilton: An American Musical.*

Throughout my training, though, I planned on finishing the marathon listening to one particular song: "Holdin' Out for a Hero" by Bonnie Tyler.

If you don't know this song, you have my permission to bookmark this page, jump onto your favorite music streaming service, search for this song, listen to it, email me at chris@chrisdtgordon.com to thank me for the suggestion, and continue reading. If you already know this song, you can take those actions, too.

There is a reason why so many movies and TV shows have paid good money to use this song. *Shrek 2, Loki,* the 2023 *Super Mario Bros.* movie, shows that aren't based on comic books, cartoons, or video games: They all used this masterpiece to crank up the tension and excitement in their respective productions. Whenever it blasted into my earholes on my runs, I felt my pace instinctively pick up and a smile creep across my face. If anything could motivate me to cross the finish line in a strong and heroic fashion, this song could!

The playlist was about 1 hour and 18 minutes long, obviously not long enough to last the entire marathon. So, after the fuel belt/ bottle exchange with the family, I also put in my earbuds, pressed "Play," and rocked out! Given my goal pace, Bonnie should've started singing sometime during the 26th mile.

That WAS the plan. Then mile 21 happened.

Even though my pace slowed in the last part of the race, the music kept playing at its regular speed. When the penultimate song in my playlist, "Feel Invincible" by Skillet, ended in the middle of mile 24, I stopped the music. I couldn't change the last few miles, but I could control the last two. I pushed myself past other runners on the slightly winding bike path until I reached that bridge. Then I resumed the music.

Once that synthesizer and those drums kicked in, I blocked out the pain radiating from my bottom half. Bonnie's raspy vocals generated a much-needed fire within me, and I started feeling the wind in the face again. As I approached a much younger runner who was shuffling forward, I barked at him to get going. He (let's call him Sir Pipsy Shufflington III, Shuffly for short) picked up his pace and momentarily blasted in front of me. I didn't care about passing Shuffly. I now had enough motivation for the both of us.

This cat-and-mouse game, Shuffly slowing down until I yelled at him to run again, continued until the final turn, which curved up and to the right until the sidewalk joined Civic Center Drive. The song's crescendo from the bridge to the third chorus exploded as I saw the large blue inflatable signifying the end of my journey and quickly reached a speed my body had no business running at that moment. I glanced to my right briefly as I crossed the finish line mat.

(Photo courtesy of Ben Garvin/@marathonmoment)

3:16:56!

I did it! Despite those last six miles of trial and tribulation, I completed my goal of finishing the marathon in under 3 hours and 20 minutes. As I clopped my feet to a stop and pounded fists with Shuffly (he'd already finished at that point), a sense of peace washed over me. I actually ran a marathon about a half hour faster than when I was "whole" and nine years younger. For years I had told people that I was just bad at the marathon, that it would take me almost a decade to prepare my body for 26.2 miles of running. In reality, I just needed the right training, the proper mindset, and five months to do it.

I also needed to sit down because my feet were KILLING ME!

I scooted my livid feet towards the nice young lady who looped my finisher's medal around my neck, and I thanked her. Then I just stood there. And stood there some more. And kept up that tradition until another young lady (this one wearing a Mayo Clinic badge) asked me if I needed some help. I graciously took her arm as she led me to the post-race treat table. I grabbed a bottle of Muscle Milk, a couple Gatorades, and not enough bananas and scooted towards the exit where I saw Becky, the kids, and Bill. We chatted for a bit, and Bill graciously took our picture. Becky knew that I like to hang out after races to chat with other runners, so she took Bill and the kids back to the house and waited for me to call for a ride (I was NOT walking there). I also saw two more colleagues, Darla and Tracy, who had cheered me on as I crossed the finish line; they even took a cool picture of me looking strong in my final push. A minute later, I heard my name called from behind me, and I gingerly turned around.

Blake walked over to me. He told me that, after his pit stop, he returned to his pace and finished the race two minutes behind me. Given where he started on his running journey, his performance was an impressive accomplishment. It'll only be a matter of time before he runs a BQ, too.

All in all, my marathon attempt was a successful venture. I am disappointed that, due to a record number of qualified entrants, my marathon time was not good enough to get me into Boston for the 2024 race. The additional cutoff time turned out to be five minutes and 29 seconds, which means one had to run 5:29 under their gender and age time requirement to gain entry into the field of 30,000. I ran with only three minutes and four seconds to spare. However, my gratitude and resilience motivated me to immediately register for the Lake Wobegon Trail Marathon, a rather fast course that I will run on May 4th; I might just wear a Star Wars shirt to signify the occasion. I'll probably also use "The Force is with me, and I am with the Force" as a running mantra.

I AM comforted by the fact that I can now run a marathon reasonably well. Officially, I finished 17th overall at Med City, and I placed 2nd in my age division. I'm proud of how the first 20 miles went; I kept a strong, consistent pace throughout and didn't allow anyone to pass me. In my next marathon training cycle, I will focus more on maintaining my pace in the last quarter of the race, but I actually like having something specific to improve rather than just "get better at running," so I'm good with that.

PASS ON PERFECTION AND GO FOR GREATNESS!

I HAVE A FAVORITE PHRASE, actually a mantra, that I like to share with others: "Pass on perfection and go for greatness!" I end every episode of my podcast, *Scar Bearers*, with that line because it aptly reflects how I try to live my life.

Ever since my hospitalization, any hope of having a "perfect" body flew right out the open window of the ICU room. The upper right side of my body looks like Anakin Skywalker at the end of *Revenge of the Sith*. I could go as a topographical map for Halloween. I have a chunk of my left leg on my right arm. I'm missing an entire thigh muscle AND a nipple. Whenever I go swimming, I can feel people looking at my scars. I could cover up my scars and the thand, but that doesn't make them disappear. To this day, I have a line of stiffness that runs from my right thumb to my forearm.

That doesn't even include the physical struggle that skin grafts present. Since they are nonporous, they do not sweat. That means they don't release body heat. Imagine taking a roll of cellophane and wrapping it tightly around your right arm, shoulder, chest, and back. Now leave the cellophane on your body...forever. That's what skin grafts feel like on the inside.

On the outside, they BARELY feel. Skin grafts contain far

fewer nerve endings than normal skin. My kids routinely play a game called "Hey Dad, can you feel this?," where they poke my skin grafts with varying degrees of pressure to test my sensitivity. When I go sledding with my kids, I need to pay attention to my right elbow. Once, I sledded down the hill with Seth on my back, and we hit a jump. We landed; nothing hurt, so we kept sledding. Later that day, I removed my sweatshirt, and my left hand felt wetness on my right elbow.

"Why is my elbow wet?" I first asked. Then I looked at my hand.

"Why is my hand red?" I second asked, as I saw blood smeared on my fingers.

Occasionally, when we're getting ready for bed, Becky asks, "When did you get those?"

"Those what?"

"This," she replies as she touches random points on my back, "and this…oh, and this one."

So, I scoff at the overall pursuit of perfection.

When you think about it, though, virtually every "perfect" image in society today is fleeting at best and usually a fabrication. The model in the magazine ad, the car on the billboard, the perfectly grilled hamburger with the perfectly balanced condiments in the commercial: Each of those examples was meticulously manufactured just for that one photograph or seconds-long video. However, how long will that model hold that pose? How many miles before that car gets a ding or a scratch? Is that hamburger even edible?!?

Instead of pursuing perfection, focus on achieving greatness! It lasts much longer, and let's face it, it's more pleasant to hang out with a great person than a "perfect" one.

USING MY VOICE

As I resumed my life post-hospitalization, I felt an increasing need to use my experience to inspire and motivate others. My recovery from this rare situation exceeded everyone's expectations, and several family members, friends, and strangers repeatedly stated that I could help people. Occasionally, I spoke to a Health class in Becky's school whenever they reached their disease unit. However, I didn't immediately pursue motivational speaking; instead, I tried my hand at online fitness coaching. I won't spend much of your time on this short chapter of my journey, as I don't wish to unintentionally cast shade on this type of endeavor. Ultimately, it just wasn't a good fit for me. I felt that my story and message would always need to take a backseat to the coaching, and I didn't have the skill or time to do both. I did learn how to use social media more effectively, and I adopted a breakfast practice of taking a morning protein shake that I still follow to this day. So, it wasn't an entire waste.

On January 1, 2020, I decided to pursue the path that actually led me to write this very book: Public speaking. I could not keep my story and message to myself; too many people needed to hear and benefit from it. It helped that I don't fear speaking in public. If anything, I have always loved the challenge and the energy I've gained from performing in front of others, whether I'm on a theater stage, reading in front of a congregation, or belting out my favorite songs during a karaoke session (to the detriment of others, that last one is).

What should I say, though? I knew that just sharing my story wouldn't have that much effect. Sure, people might find my survival and decision to live life to the fullest inspiring. That said, as a veteran teacher, I knew I had to have an actual message to share. After all, millions of people have death-defying tales of trials and triumph to tell; what would make MY story any different from theirs? How could I separate myself from them?

It actually didn't take long to answer those questions. I thought back to that fateful conversation Becky and I had in the hospital when she told me about the wonderful things people were doing for us. I remembered thinking about how many things in my life I was thankful to have (not just the big things, but the small ones, as well). I remembered counting how many wonderful people I had in my life that had a positive impact on me and my family. I remembered brainstorming how I could help others be thankful by doing nice things for them. While I considered those memories, I connected with my teacher/writer side to create a name or acronym. That's when I landed on "The Attitude of Gratitude," or TAG.

TAG works so well as a concept on numerous levels. First of all, I love using catchy writing tactics like rhyming. Secondly, I have an elementary teaching license and years of experience working with kids. Tag is a timeless playground game with natural appeal, so using the name of that game to identify my speaking message was kismet. Thirdly, I wanted my speaking message to not only benefit the participants in the audience, but I also want them to help those in their respective social circles, even strangers.

So, by "numerous," I meant three. But they're three REALLY GOOD levels.

However, I felt that I needed to start out speaking on a concept that people knew about, even if Tag is an extremely popular game. So, I chose the SMART goal concept, but I modified it by adding "Re" at the end. Yes, I spoke on the "SMARTRe" method of setting goals, but why the "Re" at the end? I wanted to differentiate it from the SMART method; subconsciously, though, I think I wanted to also attract Canadian audiences.

I also needed to actually find a stage to share my story and message. At that time, I had already absorbed information from a few different podcasts and professional speakers, and they all stated that "if you can't find a stage to speak on, create your own." Thankfully, my church had a large fellowship hall, and Pastor Bode allowed me to use the space for free. So, I scheduled my talk for 6:30 PM on February 25, 2020, posted multiple times on my social media channels, and even asked the church to advertise my presentation, "Go for Greatness" on their popular roadside sign.

Twenty-five attendees, mostly friends and a few kind strangers, showed up on the 25th. They took notes on the premade sheets I placed on the tables, they laughed (more or less) at my jokes, and they all had positive and/or constructive criticism for my performance. A few of them had never heard my story and expressed their admiration and appreciation. After the last attendee left the building, I stood in the empty fellowship hall and smiled; I could see myself doing this much more often. I couldn't wait for my next speaking opportunity!

Three weeks later:

Now, I am not a "Why me?" type of person, but I certainly recognize irony when I see it. When the world started shutting down due to the COVID-19 pandemic, I was bummed that the slight momentum I built when speaking at my church fizzled out. However, I wasn't disheartened about speaking. I knew I needed to speak, and no pandemic was going to stop me. I just needed a different stage.

Enter the podcast. Millions worldwide discovered how to pivot their energies to survive or thrive in this new reality (Doordash, anyone?), and I was no different. I was immediately excited about starting my own podcast. I could now own that stage, and no one could take it from me. Even if no one else listened, I still had a way to take some reps. That said, I needed people to listen so I could get some feedback. At the time that I started my podcast, which I called

Scar Bearers, I had roughly 800 Facebook friends. So, in my infinite social media wisdom, I thought, "Awesome! I'm already starting with 800 subscribers! Once I tell them about the podcast, things will really take off!"

I can hear your laughter, you know.

Amazingly enough, telling people that you have a podcast is like telling them you have COVID; they want to stay as far away as possible! You would've thought I'd learned my lesson when I tried the fitness coaching thing, but this was different. I wasn't trying to sell anything except my story, hope, and inspiration. What's wrong with that?!?

Well, truth be told, I still don't have 800 subscribers as I pen this book. I did figure out one thing very quickly after starting my podcast, though; I could only stretch out MY story for so many episodes. I needed to feature others' stories and tell their tales of trial and triumph.

THANK YOU, INTERNET!

Before I started the podcast, I had connected with several fellow necrotizing fasciitis (NF) survivors through Facebook. One of them was a six-year-old boy who lost his leg and participated in wheelchair basketball. His mother and I had communicated occasionally through posts and Instant Messenger, so I felt comfortable approaching her.

The upside of featuring a younger person for your first interview is that they don't really know how a good interview should go. His mother appeared with him in the interview, which I appreciated for two reasons.

1) He could feel more comfortable throughout the experience.

2) I could feel more comfortable throughout the experience.

With all firsts, I learned a lot. One big lesson I learned is to know how your equipment works before you use it. We had a recording issue which essentially erased our entire conversation. Whoopsies! I took really good notes, though, so I offered a play-by-play of the interview for the episode.

After a few more interviews, I decided to incorporate a tool I had only used once before the pandemic: YouTube. When the world screeched to a halt, I made some short videos for teachers who needed help adjusting to teaching online, as well as a running documentary that detailed my effort to run the Goldy's 10 Mile virtually. Those videos were on my phone, though, and I didn't want to interview people on my phone (no disrespect to those who do; I just am not comfortable with it).

I started using Zoom, and instantly I increased my reach by 100% (which for me meant 20 more people would probably see my episodes). Over time I've changed various aspects of the podcast, such as the podcast theme song (thanks, Nate!), the thumbnail look, and how I've incorporated a bit of TAG into one of my final questions. For a while I also brought on a production assistant, Nate's son Britton, whose technical skill surpassed my own and took the videos to another level.

Something I've kept pretty constant is my interview style; I've allowed the guest to tell their story with little interruption from me until they give me a definite pause or use an undefined term or phrase that might go over the viewer's head. I've tried to put myself in the viewer's shoes and think, "If I don't know what ________ means, the average viewer may not know what it means." I've found that it makes the guest more relatable. Again, I don't have tons of listeners/subscribers, but I want the ones I do have to know I value them and want them to get the most out of each episode.

While I worked on my own podcast, I also discovered that other people needed guests for THEIR podcasts, and my story appealed to many of those stages. THIS is how I really honed my speaking message! I chatted with fellow podcasters from across the country and certain areas around the world. In 2021 I even spoke to a group of Nepalese high school students…at 5AM my time! I don't recommend doing that all the time, but it was a memorable experience to connect with young people halfway around the world from the comfort of my basement while most of my hemisphere slept.

I have met so many fantastic people with some amazing stories through podcasts! I haven't made any money directly from *Scar Bearers*, but between the repetitions I've taken on others' stages and featuring others' tales on my own, I have grown as a speaker and a person. Someday, perhaps, I can secure a sponsor or two and make some money from the podcast; if I do, though, I want a dark chocolate manufacturer to sponsor me (podcasts often advertise services they profess using, and I go through quite a bit of dark chocolate…that, and Transformers).

My pursuit to speak professionally has also increased my website designing skills when I created www.chrisdtgordon.com. I am also proud to say that I have officially designed my own T-shirts (though my friend and professional artist Jim Arendt cleaned up the graphics beautifully). By the way, one of my favorite shirts is on the right and features the last question I ask my podcast guests. It's also an homage to my childhood obsession with dinosaurs.

As I'm typing right now, I have about a dozen professional speaking engagements under my belt, with at least a half dozen more on the schedule. I'm also participating in a virtual speaking cohort to level up my business, presentation, and marketing skills. While I have loved teaching (especially teaching from my own home, which has prepared me for entrepreneurship more than I realize), I am uniquely qualified to deliver my story and message. I need to step up and deliver; the world needs more gratitude, positivity, and resilience. The world needs me…and you!

RUNNER'S WORLD

Besides reaching out on live and virtual stages, I also put my fingers to the keyboard and shared my story and message in print (to which you're likely reading this and thinking, "Duh!"). I've written a couple magazine and blog articles, and I've even contributed to a couple personal development anthologies. Even before I started to speak, though, there was one publication where I really wanted to find my story: *Runner's World* magazine.

Running Helped Me Recover From a Life-Altering Infection
AS TOLD TO EMILY SHIFFER

(Photo courtesy of @carolineyangphoto)

If you're not familiar, *Runner's World* is a very well-known and renowned running-based publication. For years it has featured stories and articles that have informed and entertained runners of every athletic level, from beginner to Olympic-level.

I had reached out to the magazine on a few

occasions in the past, but I never received the response I wanted. If I were in a different mindset, I would've given up and moved on. However, I NEEDED to share my message with my fellow runners, and this magazine could help me do that.

(Photo courtesy of @carolineyangphoto)

Finally, I received an email from Emily Shiffer, a *Runner's World* staff writer in Fall 2021. Emily sent me a list of questions about my story and how running played a part in it. I spent the next two hours crafting my answers; I was so focused on my responses that I think I missed dinner that evening. The writer also reached out to a Twin Cities-based photographer, Caroline Yang, who scheduled to meet with me on a November Saturday morning. Caroline asked me where we should meet; I told her that New Ulm has a big hill that overlooks the town and that would be a great place for pictures.

Caroline and her assistant Mallory pulled into the Hermann Park parking lot on that brisk November morning. After gifting them each with a case of 1919 Root Beer (proudly made in New Ulm), we discussed what shots we should take. Now, as we stated before, I am a huge geek. I also love a good cape (sorry, Edna Mode), and I own a few of them. I knew that I wanted to wear a cape in one of the pictures; thankfully, Caroline was willing to go with it.

So, I took off my shirt and donned my big red cape. My skin grafts insulated the right side of my body, but my left side was NOT happy with me. To appease my body, I put on my knitted TAG hat and running gloves, and I jumped around and did pushups between shots to increase my body heat. Unfortunately, we didn't have a strong headwind, so Mallory graciously threw the cape up so Caroline could capture the image on the left side of this paragraph.

After she took the cape picture, Caroline asked me what else I had in mind. I told her about an idea I had that stemmed from one of my favorite actors, Ryan Reynolds. While I jokingly referred to myself as a discount Deadpool, a poster from another one of his movies, *Free Guy*, stuck with me. On the poster, Ryan (we're on a first-name basis) looked blissfully towards the upper left corner of the frame while chaos reigned behind him. It just spoke to me.

Again, Caroline was game, so I struck an exaggeratedly energetic running pose and slapped the silliest look on my face.

Caroline nailed it!

On New Year's Eve 2021, that *Runner's World* issue arrived at my brother Mark's house; we were visiting for Christmas, and he's a subscriber. I was over the moon with excitement! Emily and Caroline combined their talents to craft a fantastic article that I love sharing with people. That article has led to a few new connections, including a couple of those who really appreciated my story and found it very inspirational…which was its intended purpose.

YOU CAN'T SPELL "COSPLAYER" WITHOUT "SCAR"

You might presume that me wearing a cape in a nationally recognized magazine would indicate that I like to wear costumes. You would be correct. I love dressing up in costumes, or "cosplaying." Cosplaying takes the act of wearing a Halloween costume to the next level. There exists several levels of skill when it comes to cosplay; I hover in the bottom levels of the cosplay skill scale. I've made a few small parts of a costume, but I usually buy the clothing and materials and doctor them to best fit that character. I also have very skilled friends who do the heavy lifting (sewing, hemming, crafting masks, etc.). Still, I love it!

In 2014 John (the giant) invited me to accompany him to a comic book convention called Salt Lake Comic Con (SLCC) which was held at the Salt Palace Convention Center in Salt Lake City, Utah. If you're not familiar with comic book conventions (or cons), actual comic books are just one facet of these events. Cons encompass almost every corner of popular fandoms: Comic books, regular books, movies, TV shows, video games, board games, social media, etc. You might find something sports-related, but you have to look for it. At cons, geek is chic!

Perhaps the most beloved form of participation at cons is cosplaying. The entire spectrum of cosplay skill is on display at a con, ranging from someone wearing a shirt that reads, "This is my cosplay" to 10-foot-tall, fully movable mechanized suits of armor, complete with working lights and sound effects that reflect years of expert craftsmanship and love for the subject manner. No matter your level of cosplay skill, cosplay is a wonderful way for con attendees to share their fandom love and connect with others (as long as respect is shown).

John was selling his books at a booth at SLCC, and he invited me as a 40th birthday present. At the time his most popular book was *Failstate*, a young adult novel based on a teenager (Failstate) with destructive powers. The powers deformed his face when they were activated, so he would wear a black mask and hood. He also wore black gauntlet gloves, a black hoodie, gray camouflage pants, and black combat boots: All items that could be purchased online, my optimal skill of cosplay construction.

I brought my Failstate costume to SLCC and had a great time interacting with other cosplayers (who had no idea who I was, but that's OK). I even met Stan Lee dressed as Failstate for a photo opportunity. Like the cosplayers, Stan had no idea who I was supposed to be, but at least John can show others that Failstate met Stan Lee.

A year after my hospitalization, I felt the urge to return to SLCC, but I didn't just want to go. I wanted to have a fantastic time! To accomplish that goal, I first recruited a partner-in-crime: Dave. He lived in Helena, Montana, and while it might have saved time to fly to SLCC separately, we decided that I would fly into Helena on a Wednesday night and road trip through the night to arrive in Salt Lake City on Thursday morning just in time to get in line for a panel starring Mark Hamill (Luke Skywalker, Joker from *Batman: the*

Animated Series, and many other projects). The panel was so popular that it had to take place in the Vivint Smart Home Arena, now called the Delta Center.

After the panel, Dave and I checked into our hotel room and prepared our cosplay. From the conception of our plan, I decided that my cosplay had to incorporate my skin grafts and scars, and while I jokingly refer to myself as a discount Deadpool, I only had one character in mind: Wolverine.

Wolverine, another Marvel superhero, is known mainly for his healing factor and his adamantium claws. My skin grafts and scars handled the healing factor details, and I used ripped clothes and fake blood around them to make it look like I had just fought someone. I actually made the claws by shaving down wooden stir sticks and glued them onto wooden dollies, and then I spray painted them silver (I was a level above the T-shirt guy). Wolverine also sports a unique hairstyle and mutton chops, so I bought a black wig, some mousse for styling the wig, and mascara for the outlandish sideburns. Dave dressed as an internet character called Dr. McNinja, which was another inexpensive costume.

Once we entered the Salt Palace, we beelined it to the Mark Hamill photo opportunity line. We worked out the photo details as we snaked closer to Mark, including using a burned mannequin hand in a Star Wars inside joke. We also noticed that the photo ops team created a lightning-fast turnover, moving people through the photo process like a well-oiled machine. This meant we wouldn't have much time to chat with Mark AND nail our intended poses, so we chose to sacrifice any long-winded gushings of admiration and get right to the pose.

If it's unclear what's happening, I cut off Dr. McNinja Dave's "hand" and gave it to Mark/Luke to replace the one he lost in *Empire Strikes Back*. Dave used a red sock to create the stump look. I think he nailed it! Kudos also to Mark for the impromptu shocked look.

I wore my Wolverine cosplay throughout the rest of SLCC. While some people complimented me on my fantastic "makeup," a few eagle-eyed attendees correctly identified the skin grafts and commended me on making the most of my situation. One person even gave me a hug for my bravery. I also entered the cosplay contest just to see how well I could do. As expected, I was WAY out of my league, but Ro Malaga, the MC of the cosplay contest, gifted me and Dave some really good seats to another popular celebrity panel.

All in all, the weekend was a rousing success! Dave and I made some fun memories, and I learned that using my skin grafts and scars for cosplay worked well aesthetically and as an inspiration for others to share their own scars and not just hide them.

I returned to Salt Lake City six years later in 2022 with another friend, Mack, a fellow NF survivor whom I first met as a *Scar Bearers* podcast guest. Not only did I choose another scar-bearing cosplay (Strong Bad), I also had the honor and fortune to share TAG as a presenter while dressed as One Punch Man, another favorite cosplay of mine.

I also met Kevin Smith, another extremely beloved comic book icon, which was cool.

PLAY TAG WITH ME!

THIS IS THE PART WHERE you take some action. I had learned at a young age that playing Tag alone is boring and embarrassing (true story). Playing Tag with others, however, is fun and exciting; plus, the more people playing, the better! Just as Superman needs the Justice League to help him keep the world safe, I can't make the world a better place by myself; I need your help!

The second half of this book is a six-month journal that you can use to track how much you play TAG every day. The first, middle, and final pages of the journal are assessments (we teachers LOVE our assessments, you know) where you can gauge your level of gratitude. Each of the other pages contains a box for every day of the week. You decide when YOUR week starts; I'm a Sunday-first kind of guy, but I know many people who treat Monday as the first day of their week. Additionally, I created weekly journal prompts that challenge you to increase your gratitude in different ways. What's truly important is that you use practice TAG daily.

A 2017 article from *Greater Good Magazine* states that people who make it a point to count their blessings tend to be happier and less depressed[1]. What's more, one of the studies mentioned in the article featured about 300 people who'd sought mental health counseling. The study recruited the participants just before their first counseling session, and they reported, on average, clinically low levels of mental health. The participants were split into three groups (while they still went to counseling sessions): One group did nothing except attend counseling sessions, another group journaled about their deepest feelings and ideas about negative experiences in their lives, and the last wrote a letter of gratitude to another person once a week for three weeks. The study concluded with the letter group experiencing significantly better mental health results than the other two groups, and they only practiced gratitude for a short time[1]. Imagine the changes you could experience when you practice gratitude for an entire six months!

I could share other studies to drive home the importance of gratitude, but I feel my own examples are more significant.

T– THINK ABOUT THE GOOD THINGS IN YOUR LIFE.

Every day I constantly think about things I am grateful to own or can access. I often mention my affinity for door hinges, my duct taped mouse, and my skin grafted armpit (which has halved my deodorant usage and is a fun conversation piece…at least for me).

THE LITTLE BLUE PEBBLE

In March 2022 Becky and I took the kids to Florida to experience

Disney World, Universal Studios, and the ocean. The kids had never been south of Missouri, so it was quite the adventure for them.

On our first full day in the parks, we went to Magic Kingdom and did lots of "Magic Kingdom" things: Got our picture taken in front of Cinderella's castle; jumped on the "Pirates of the Caribbean" ride; rode and were slightly splashed on Splash Mountain. After lunch, though, Becky and I decided to head back to the All-Star Music Resort (our home for the week) and throw the kids into the pool. Once we changed into our suits, the kids and I headed down to the guitar-shaped pool right by our room while Becky took a well-deserved nap.

We jumped into the refreshing water and immediately felt bad for our family and friends back up north…for about five seconds. It almost blew the kids' minds that they were swimming outside in March! About 15 minutes passed, and the kids saw others their age and asked to play with them. I happily let them play and decided to get out of the water for a minute. I, too, relished the idea of being warm while outside in winter, so I stood around and basked in the sunlight. I don't like wearing a shirt when I swim, so my skin grafts were on full display.

Fun fact: Most people don't usually approach shirtless strangers who are missing a nipple. So, I knew that no one was going to talk to me. Taking advantage of my temporary freedom, I hopped back into the pool.

I dove underwater (all of five feet) to inspect the pool floor. It was white concrete embedded with myriad pebbles of many different colors. After a few seconds, my gaze fell upon a royal blue speck. I thought about where it came from, how long it had been there, how cool it was that, out of all the pools in all the resorts in Disney World, that I am looking only at this particular pebble, and that no one else in the world will likely ever notice this one tiny rock. No matter if we ever go back to that resort or not, I will always cherish that little blue pebble for being a part of that memory.

When I think about that trip to Florida, the memory of the little blue pebble uniquely stands out. It doesn't stand out because it was extraordinarily fun, emotional, or because I made it with other people. Rather, it was a moment of near complete serenity. No one else was aware that I was having that experience, so I had no distractions pulling me away. In fact, the excitement and noise of the other swimmers faded into muffled white noise, which blended with the coolness of the water to envelope me in an aquatic chamber of peace. For that 15 or 20 seconds, I possessed that chamber of peace in the middle of a crowded pool in one of the busiest, most energetic places on the Eastern Seaboard, if not the entire continent…and it was brilliant.

Unfortunately, I cannot transport you to that pool to find that little blue pebble. However, you can find your own.

Mission: Pick a spot to focus on for at least 15-20 seconds, letting all other stimuli and distractions fall into the background. Try to imagine what the spot's perspective would look like, as if it were your own eye. Take a few deep breaths during this time to calm yourself (unless you're underwater and not scuba diving or snorkeling). Note: Do not attempt this while operating a vehicle or performing surgery.

THE 5-IN-10

A couple paragraphs ago, I mentioned that I constantly think about items that I already own that I appreciate. I actively think about how the most pedestrian, ordinary household item holds value for me, whether it be a paperclip, the eyelets in your shoes, or a light bulb.

One quick and (mildly) challenging way I do this is "the 5-in-10." At any given point during the day, I give myself 10 seconds to select five items around me. After selecting the five items, I must explain why each item has value to me. I explain each item's significance out loud so the meaning resonates with me for a longer amount of time.

Since I started practicing this activity, my appreciation for the items constantly around me has grown exponentially. It also has helped me decide what I can keep in the house or what I can donate to charity or just throw away (which Becky appreciates).

Mission: I challenge you to start using the 5-in-10 in your home, at work, on your commute, especially at the beginning of the day. What better way to start the day than to immediately appreciate what is all around you!

Also, when you find yourself having negative thoughts about a personal or professional situation, use the 5-in-10 to regain proper perspective. I often do this when several job-based projects are thrust upon me at once. Instead of bemoaning those extra duties, I quickly list 5 positive aspects of my job that align with those tasks. Usually, I actually perform those activities better when I find something to appreciate about them.

GRATITUDE GLASSES

For the 5-in-10 to work, you must see positive things around you. For some people, that's easy to do; for others, it might be a struggle. Those who struggle might need an additional tool to make the 5-in-10 work. That's where my friend Ryan Reynolds comes in.

Besides being Deadpool and an all-around great guy, Ryan also starred in that movie *Free Guy* which I mentioned before. In the movie he plays Guy, a non-playable character (NPC) in a video game, who finds a pair of special glasses during a gameplay session. When he puts on the glasses, his entire world explodes before his eyes (not literally)! He sees all kinds of video game items that a regular player would: Health boxes, weapons, power-ups, side missions… His existence entirely changes because of those glasses (literally). If it didn't, the movie would be extremely boring.

While we are not characters in a video game, we can adorn our own gratitude glasses and see the world in a new way. Actually, I prefer the term "goggles" to "glasses," so I'll be using that term from now on.

GRATITUDE GOGGLES

When you put on your gratitude goggles, you will see items all around you that you value, even if you don't own them. Value is a matter of appreciation. Someone could wear a T-shirt that makes you smile, read a road sign that warns you of a detour, or witness an act of kindness; each of those items can add value to your day IF you allow it to happen.

Now, gratitude goggles don't erase negative things from your view. Obstacles don't disappear, and things you don't like don't evaporate into thin air. However, the positive items in your view become more noticeable and prevalent.

What's more, you can wear your gratitude goggles at any time and anywhere: At home, at school, at work. They go with any outfit, and no prescription is needed. However, people may notice you're wearing them because your outward appearance may reflect how you feel inside.

Mission: Put on your gratitude goggles when you are facing a tough situation. Locate what or who can brighten your day, help you overcome the situation, or make the situation easier to handle.

SPIN IT!

Of course, as we are only human, there are things in the world that we don't particularly like or appreciate. As agreeable as we may be, not everything fits our fancy. However, our world can be extremely divisive; many people view the world in black-or-white, good or bad. Something is either the best or the worst.

So, what can we do about those things that we don't like and avoid leading such a binary existence?

The answer: Spin it!

"Spinning a story" means changing a story so it fits a particular narrative in a more flattering and/or less damaging way. The spin might involve making some parts of the story more important, downplaying other details, and/or omitting some pieces altogether.

Instead of making the view more divisive, though, the goal here is to create more shades of gray so we can reprogram ourselves (and help others) to develop more social connectivity. We can spin how we see or feel about something we do not appreciate or like. For example, I am not a fan of mint-flavored food for the most part, Andes mints being the exception. I tolerate the flavor of my toothpaste because I like my teeth. However, Becky and the kids love making mint chocolate chip cookies together, and I love seeing them making those memories, as well. Also, when I train for a marathon, I try to eat as few sweets as possible, even though her regular chocolate chip cookies are the best in the world! So those mint cookies even help me out in that way.

Another example is *The Fast and The Furious* movie franchise. I have never seen any of those movies, and I don't plan to do so. However, I appreciate that other people like those films. Also, each movie employs thousands of people for jobs such as set construction, makeup, costumes, car maintenance (I'm assuming), video effects, and other areas of moviemaking. Additionally, the *Fast/Furious*-verse has propelled several actors into superstardom, like Gal Gadot (Wonder Woman). Which *F/F* movie was she in? Don't ask me! I just know she was in one of them and apparently did a good job.

Mission: Choose something you don't like and find at least three positive aspects about it. Then share those discoveries with someone else, like on social media, a text, or a conversation, and challenge them to do the same.

A– ACKNOWLEDGE THE APPRECIATED.

I sometimes embarrass my kids when we're in public and I talk with everyone. OK, not literally everyone, but at least the employees of the establishments we patronize. I call them by name if I know it or can see their name tag clearly, I ask them how their day is going, and I thank them for their help (even if they couldn't ultimately successfully help me). I want each person I encounter to know that I appreciate them for two reasons:

1) Every person has value no matter how we're connected or what job they possess;

2) The more people see that you appreciate it when they do a kind task, the more likely that they'll do it again.

One example of this very phenomenon occurs at the beginning of each school year. My virtual school is physically housed in Houston, MN, and partners with the onsite public school. Every year we virtual teachers head to Houston for a couple days of in-person training, which includes having breakfast in the high school cafeteria. Being from Michigan, I was raised with putting ketchup on my scrambled eggs because I'm a civilized person. 😉 People in Minnesota have not caught onto this quite yet, so when I asked Robin, the lovely kitchen supervisor for some ketchup for my eggs during my first year at the school, she was taken aback and apologized that she didn't have any ready. I thanked her for her consideration and went on my way.

The next year, though, when I walked up to the counter to get my breakfast, Robin exclaimed, "I remembered!" and excitedly held up a bottle of ketchup. I was so pleasantly surprised that I thanked her at least three times! Every year afterwards, she had ketchup ready for me whenever they served eggs for breakfast.

I didn't have the heart to tell her I also put peanut butter on my pancakes.

DAD AND THE NINTENDO WORLD CHAMPIONSHIPS

There is no time limit to acknowledge someone. In fact, the person you are acknowledging doesn't even need to be alive. One of my most vivid memories of my dad came at one of my most potentially embarrassing moments.

In 1990, Nintendo was the undisputed king of home video game consoles and had started a worldwide event called "The Nintendo World Championships." Competitions were held in cities across the US; one such competition was held in Cobo Arena in Detroit, MI, about 90 miles south of my hometown of Clio.

Being huge video game fans, my best friend Chris and I decided that we NEEDED to compete in the NWC; however, I was only 15 at the time and Chris couldn't get a car to drive. So, my dad (along with my brother Jeff) drove us down to Detroit to enter the competition. I don't remember how much admission was to enter the event, but each attempt cost $5. Chris' parents gave him some money, and I'd earned some cash from babysitting; we were good to go!

We knew that every contestant would play sections of three games (*Super Mario Bros.*, *Rad Racer*, and *Tetris*), and one needed to earn enough points within a time span of six minutes and 21 seconds to advance to the semifinals.

Admittedly Chris was a better gamer than I, and he advanced to the semis on his first attempt. Meanwhile, I struggled with the *Rad Racer* portion and didn't make the cut. I was determined to join him, so I started playing that section of the competition over and over in my head as we grabbed some Little Caesars pizza for lunch. I scarfed down my two slices so I could get back in line, anxious to prove myself. I loved video games, this was my time to shine, and I was determined to leave it all on the competition floor.

As I inched closer back to the stand-up arcade cabinets, the crowd grew from a few hundred people in the morning to a couple thousand, all eager to achieve the same goal as I. Sure, they could really like video gamers, too, I thought, but they could advance next year. I'm going to give them a show that they won't soon forget!

Finally, I was the next person to step up to one of the cabinets. The heat emanating from the crowd caused me to sweat a bit. My nerves washed over me as I approached the machine, and I held true to my word.

I left it all on the competition floor…and the screen, and the joystick, and the buttons.

My fellow gamers collectively gasped as I threw up the pizza and pop I had just consumed and collapsed against the cabinet. I don't know whether the pizza was bad or my nerves had gotten the better of me, but one thing was certain: I was done for the day.

I was less certain about the next few minutes, but I do remember Dad walking me out of the second floor bathroom after he washed me up. Jeff later said that Dad had basically swept me up and carried me like a baby up the stairs. Mind you, I wasn't a big kid (about 5'3", around 120 lbs.), but I was still a teenager. Still, Dad (who was 6'1") took charge and handled the situation before anything else happened.

The four of us walked back to our 1984 Buick LeSabre, where I crawled into the back seat and assumed the fetal position during the ride home. Dad never really brought it up to me afterwards; he knew that I was disappointed and definitely wasn't planning on throwing up in front of hundreds of people. He just did the dad thing, took care of the situation, and moved on.

I "think" I thanked him at some point; if I didn't then, I really can't say anything to him now. What I can do is follow his example and acknowledge him by helping my kids when they're in a similar situation by taking charge and doing what he had done for me.

Someone else I needed to acknowledge is Chris. When we left Cobo that afternoon, he effectively forfeited his entry into the semifinals. Again, I don't remember if I ever shared my appreciation verbally, but decades later I found a way to share how I felt. I had discovered a person on Facebook who creates systems that store and play thousands of retro video games and bought one of the systems for myself. It worked like a dream (and still does), so I secretly ordered one for Chris. He messaged me after receiving it, and I explained why I bought it for him. He hadn't given that moment at Cobo much thought after it happened, but he still thanked me profusely for the system and still enjoys it to this day.

THE TRIPLE A

Thinking about Kris, the head nurse, during my time in the hospital and how she was able to recognize my favorite movie at a random garage sale when she probably had so many other things on her mind prompted me to explore the notion of seeing people for who they are apart from our direct connection to them. That was the impetus for the Triple A.

The Triple A prompts you to "Actively Augment your Appreciation" of someone with whom you share a connection. We too often view people based on how they affect us. By observing how they impact the world around THEM, we might develop a greater appreciation for having that person in our lives.

The Triple A works with anyone you know, no matter the relationship. They can be your partner, a sibling, a friend, an acquaintance, perhaps even that cashier you see at the grocery store who has a smile for every customer.

I often use Becky, my wife, as an example. Yes, she's my wife, my partner, and my best friend; without going into too much detail, we have a strong relationship. When I take myself out of the picture, though, I see her in a different light. I notice that she's a fantastic mother, a loving daughter and sister, a caring friend, a brilliant teacher, a talented musician, a great athlete, and she's almost as geeky as I am (but better at concealing it); basically, she is a wonderful asset to our various communities. After making all those observations, I then reflect on how she is MY wife, my partner, and my best friend. How fortunate am I?! (Answer: EXTREMELY!)

It can even help repair a frayed connection or strengthen your respect for someone else. Unfortunately, we can't be best friends with everyone, and we might have someone in our lives that we don't even get along with very well. However, by using the Triple A, we can view that person in a different light based on how they benefit the world around them. I'm no fortune teller, but if we all respected each other more, I'm willing to bet that the world would be a much better place.

Mission: I challenge you to pick one person in one of your social circles each day for the Triple A. Notice how your perception of that person changes when you see that person from a more positive viewpoint. You might find that you eventually pick the same person again at some point, but that's OK. People change over time, so you might find someone has become a more positive force in the world when you return to them.

G– GIVE OTHERS A REASON TO BE GRATEFUL.

To piggyback onto the A portion, I also want to give people I know or meet a reason to be grateful during or after our encounter. I WILL NOT be the only person to benefit from my experience! I have become resilient enough to earn my Black Belt in my 40s, secure another teaching license, become a professional speaker, write this book, and qualify for the Boston Marathon. Everyone deserves to have that much resilience, but many don't possess it…yet.

Some people think that you need to change who you are to be a good person. Instead, you just need to do good things to change who you are. A July 2020 article on *envolvehealth.com* entitled "The Benefits of Helping Others: Improve Your Health Through Good Deeds" outlines five health benefits that are connected to performing good deeds. The mentioned benefits include decreased stress, decreased loneliness, longer lifespan, increased happiness, and increased motivation. The article also states that the size of the kind act doesn't matter, which means everyone qualifies for this transformation[1]. Picking up trash off the ground, holding doors for others, asking how someone is doing…they all qualify!

And giving truly strengthens your community, wherever that may be. In her book *Be Seen*, Jen Gottlieb explains how giving ties directly into creating stronger social connections. By consistently helping others, you are paying into a system that will reciprocate you in kind. The trick is to give with a servant's heart with no expectation of payback[2]. So, how do we do that?!

When we fail to achieve our big goals or even achieve our daily objectives, instead of beating ourselves down, we need to pick ourselves up, give ourselves some grace, and look for the next victory (no matter how small). For example, if you fall off your diet, don't shame yourself; pick up an apple and get back on the path to healthy eating.

GIVE A LITTLE BIT, GIVE A LITTLE BIT OF YOUR TIME TO OTHERS…

Right now, hop online and Google "benefits of volunteering." Don't worry, I'll wait.

I bet you found pages upon pages of articles noting various numbers (3, 9, 10...) of benefits one can gain from volunteering. While I could refer to many of those entries here, I chose just one:

A recent article from Mayo Clinic Health System (perhaps I'm a bit partial) that discusses three health benefits one can gain from volunteering. Research stated that volunteers, especially older adults, reported better physical health and lower rates of stress, depression, and anxiety. Volunteers also discovered a greater sense of purpose serving others, and they also learned valuable skills. Finally, volunteers created new relationships and nurtured existing ones while participating in a shared activity[1].

While many people instinctively think of an urban soup kitchen when the topic of volunteerism arises, volunteering can happen almost anywhere. Here is a list of possible volunteer options:

- Give your time to your local library, stocking books or reading to young children for a story hour.
- Contact your local school and ask where they could use an extra set of hands (or kind smile).
- Coach a youth sports team or act as a team parent, performing administrative duties so the coach can just worry about practice.
- Volunteer at your house of worship (if you have one).
- Choose to volunteer at a different house of worship (yes, you can do that). You can pick an activity that doesn't conflict with your own belief system.
- Organize a regular walking group that picks up garbage you find on your different routes.
- Offer to assist local theatre productions. Tasks may include helping actors run through lines, building sets and props, working backstage, in the tech booth, ushering, or working concessions.
- If you have a downtown area in which the city plants flowers, you could water the plants.

These are just a few of the numerous ways you could give back to the community. Again, use Google to learn about other ways and where you can volunteer in your area.

WEIRD AL 2019

It may come to absolutely no surprise to you that I am a big "Weird Al" Yankovic fan. For as long as I can remember, I could recite at least one Weird Al song almost word-for-word, much to the chagrin of anyone within earshot. I firmly believe that he is one of the greatest musicians of our time, and it is an utter shame that he has yet to headline a Super Bowl halftime show!

When his website announced the 2019 "Strings Attached" tour dates, I checked to see if he would be stopping in Minnesota. As it turned out, he was playing at the Minnesota State Fair in late August, during the only Tuesday of the State Fair dates. I bought a few general admission tickets for me, my cousin Phil, and a couple friends. Then something else caught my eye: a VIP ticket that gave you backstage passes, a pizza party with other VIP guests, and a picture AND meet-and-greet with Weird Al himself! My mind harkened back to a photo that my brother John posted on Facebook of him and Al when he (Al) performed in Kansas City where John lived. I recalled feeling a twinge of jealousy and thinking, "Someday that honor will be mine...ALL MINE!" While Becky and I didn't have a great deal of disposable income lying around, we were pretty frugal about frivolous purchases, so I didn't feel too guilty shelling out the extra money for the VIP ticket.

The Minnesota State Fair always started two Thursdays before Labor Day (the first Monday in September for my international friends), which meant that the concert would occur the night of the second day of back-to-teacher workshops. I needed to travel three hours from home and stay in Houston, MN for two nights. Thankfully, my back-to-school in-person workshops finished on

Tuesday afternoon; so, after the last staff meeting, I drove up to St. Paul, stopped to briefly visit some old friends, and had Andy, the patriarch of the clan, show me a convenient parking spot within walking distance of the fairgrounds.

Once I entered the fairgrounds, I beelined to the grandstands to gather my credentials. I bought a beautifully gaudy Weird Al Hawaiian shirt, took a silly picture with a fellow VIP, and then wandered around until Phil and the others entered the arena.

(I could painstakingly explain the next few hours of the concert, but I will save us both some time and sum it up in two words: Raucous nerdiness!)

After the final encore, an usher called us VIPs to the front of the arena, where we lined up like geeky, elated cattle and shuffled through a gate and to a giant collapsible banquet hall that you would find at an outdoor wedding held in someone's backyard…a rich someone. The portable building was decked out in classical decor, complete with "marble" busts and Bach playing in the background; since this was the "Strings Attached" tour, it was only fitting to fancy up the digs a bit. About 20 round tables filled the hall, 10 chairs to a table. I sat with a group of friendly strangers, including a father-daughter duo who stated that they had seen Al eight times before and had the pictures to prove it. We also enjoyed some semi-warm pizza and pop as we awaited our turn to meet "the Weird one," and I even received the first sheet of the PETA favorite "Weasel Stomping Day."

Finally, a Victorian-era garbed usher asked us to follow him into another building where we first had our picture taken with Al, and then stepped into another line to have the freshly printed picture signed by Mr. Yankovic. As I inched closer to meeting one of my lifelong heroes, my mind raced with the different poses I could take with him. It needed to be something worth the occasion; I did not pay triple digits to just stand next to "Weird Al" Yankovic!

As the person in front of me left Al's presence, the man himself turned to me, smiled, and said, "So, what are we doing?"

In my head, I screamed, "OH MY GAW—YOU'RE 'WEIRD AL!' YOU'RE 'WEIRD AL,' AND I'M MEETING YOU! THIS! IS! AWESOME!!!!!"

Outside my head, I took a deep breath and said in my calmest voice, "I want you to hug me like you're happy to see me."

The result:

(I'm proud of myself for holding the awkward grimace.)

I don't remember the next 20 minutes; you can blame my elation or my exhaustion for my poor memory. Eventually, though, I entered the second line to officially meet Al and have him sign my picture (which you can see). Unlike the first line, I knew exactly what I was going to say.

By this time in the evening/early morning, Al had taken a seat behind a table to chat with the VIPs. I stepped up to the table and told him what to write on the photograph. He slid it back to me, and I lifted up my shirt. I shared how his music helped me smile during my hospitalization and how I have always appreciated the gifts that he's given his fans throughout the years.

And this moment is why I included this story. It was as if he and I were the only ones in the room. His attention was focused on me and only me. He didn't look around to see how long the line was. He didn't check his watch. He only looked away from my face to look at my scars. He asked me how long I was in the hospital, congratulated me on my recovery, and thanked me for my kind words and for being a fan.

He could've been an impatient jerk. He could've winced and asked me to lower my shirt. He could have made any number of commonplace, even unsavory choices, and I would've been pleased with the picture, even if his behavior were disappointing.

But he didn't. Instead, he gave me something I didn't expect: His undivided attention. "Weird Al" Yankovic challenged me to be a better person by showing me how to be fully present for someone you just met, even after midnight and after traveling all day and performing at a world-class level for three hours. If you believe that you shouldn't meet your heroes, maybe you just need better heroes.

In short, Weird Al taught me that your presence is perhaps the greatest present you can give!

BEING A FRIENDLY NEIGHBORHOOD HERO!

When I offer examples of giving others a reason to be grateful in my presentations, I usually talk about mowing my neighbors' lawns when they need a helping hand.

Throughout the summer of 2023, my neighbor's lawn always looked unkempt. He was a single guy, and I knew he worked in a city about a half hour away, so he was never much of a homebody. Over that summer, though, I NEVER saw him around. As a result of his absence, his lawn turned into a suburban field, and I worried what might happen if someone thought that the house was abandoned.

After mowing my own front lawn one late June day, I wheeled my electric lawnmower past another neighbor's lawn and mowed the overgrowth. It took me about an hour to mow the small front yard, due to the combination of the long grass and weeds and the fact that I needed to keep plugging in the mower. I am not mechanically inclined, so I gladly deal with mowing with an extension cord so I don't need to deal with a gas motor. A month later, I noticed that my neighbor's lawn was again growing out of control, so I wheeled the mower back over and mowed again.

Becky, the kids, and I took a couple short trips after that second mow. When we returned from our second adventure, I noticed that my neighbor's lawn was freshly mowed. So, I figured that his schedule had settled down.

A few days after our return, the doorbell rang. I opened the door to find my neighbor. He explained that he had been busy with his job, taking summer college courses, and renovating the house for eventual sale; as a result, the lawn wasn't touched. I expressed my relief that I wasn't overstepping literal and metaphorical boundaries by mowing his lawn, and he smiled while he explained how much he appreciated my assistance. Coincidentally, I never told him that it was me.

He then handed me this card:

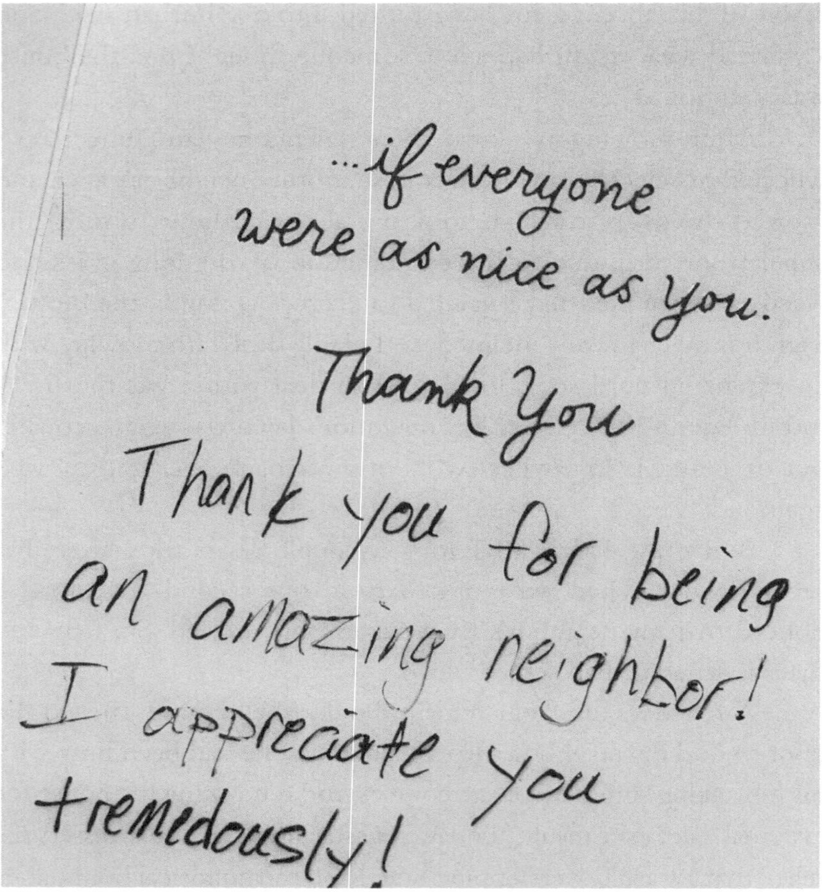

...if everyone were as nice as you.

Thank You

Thank you for being an amazing neighbor! I appreaciate you tremedously!

This is the power of TAG. Perhaps I would've noticed his overgrown lawn if my gratitude meter wasn't as elevated as it is, but that's neither here nor there. He obviously is grateful for my action, and I hope he's also to notice when someone else is in need.

Mission: I challenge you to perform one small task for someone else each day. It could be picking up a piece of trash off the ground, holding the door for someone, letting someone know that you like their shirt… You will be surprised when you discover how easy it is to make someone's day better when you think about how to make them smile.

TEACHING WITH TAG

As my hospitalization began in late March 2015 and lasted just over two months, that meant I missed the entire 4th quarter of school. Whenever I speak and tell students I missed 25% of the school year, some of them call me lucky. I wouldn't call losing a nipple being lucky, but I get where they're coming from.

That meant, though, that I didn't need to report back to work until the following August, so I could continue acclimating to my "new" body without the added pressure of teaching for a few more months. Chasing a six-year-old and three-year-old twins around the house with Becky was plenty enough for me to handle, and I took advantage of the additional opportunities to nap. When August did roll around, I was ready to get back to teaching.

Teaching online certainly offered me advantages that a traditional teaching job couldn't. For starters, since Becky dropped the kids off at their respective places, I didn't need to leave the house on a regular basis. Also, during a time when I could have lunch, I sometimes snuck in a 10- or 15-minute nap to recharge my internal battery; doing that in a brick-and-mortar classroom might have been awkward. Don't worry, admin; that only happened a few times… 😉

Teaching online is also much less physically demanding than a traditional teaching position. The classroom is contained within the computer, so I literally could stay seated all day. I didn't, though, because not only is sitting all day bad for your health, but skin grafts need to be stretched often so they don't tighten up and constrict. So, I performed exercises throughout the day; I still attended outpatient physical therapy once or twice a week until Thanksgiving 2015, so I performed the exercises that Wendy, Carol, and the others prescribed to me. I also rocked out some push-ups, pull-ups, and various yoga poses (especially downward dog) to rebuild my muscle size and tone.

One misconception many people have about online teaching is that it's much more relaxing than traditional teaching because you're not dealing with people in a face-to-face manner most of the time. It may be true; we don't come into physical contact with our students and colleagues unless it's for a social event or a professional development opportunity. However, when most of your professional impact is limited to your Internet connection, email, text messages, and a tiny window on a computer screen, things can become stressful when your WiFi goes out or a student has computer issues (either truthfully or out of avoidance).

As I encountered these issues when I returned to teaching, that was when TAG started impacting me on a professional level. Instead of wasting time on the problem itself, I first focused on the positive aspects of the situation. It could be the fact that I still had Internet service, that my students were in a safe place, and/or that I didn't have to deal with this issue with a bunch of people watching me struggle in real time.

Then I took action to remedy the situation. If any of those actions involved the assistance of someone else, I reached out to that person in a courteous manner and offered as much information as they needed to help me out. I always kept (and currently keep) the following saying in mind: "A lack of planning on your part does not equal an emergency on my part." Even if my situation was not my doing, I recognized that I was adding another task onto their plate. Offering graciousness and kindness throughout that interaction not only makes the current situation a positive experience for everyone involved, but it also increases the probability that the contacted person will offer excellent service in the future. Plus, it's just basic human decency to be nice.

Finally, I increased the number of times I gave others reasons to be grateful. Whether it be a spontaneous note of gratitude to a colleague or me choosing to play a game with a student who needed a break from the regular lessons, I intentionally acted in a way for others to feel the same positivity I did. This also included sharing my story with staff and students, which reinforced my idea to become a professional speaker.

Between my excellent recovery and the feedback I received from my speaking presentations, I became more comfortable with sharing my story and message, so I started incorporating TAG into my everyday teaching practice. In hindsight, I should have started much earlier, but I think I felt like I was "double dipping" by mixing my speaking into my teaching. In reality, this culmination was the educational Reese's Peanut Butter Cup: Two great practices that work well together. Students who are more grateful tend to be happier at school, and happy students are more likely to work more consistently on assignments. Talk about not seeing the forest for the trees!

I couldn't devote a great deal of time to it because I only had so much time to effectively teach. However, the beauty of TAG is that it can be performed in less than a minute. Also, I never expect it to catch on immediately, so working on it over time is expected.

TAG IMPLEMENTATION IDEAS FOR THE CLASSROOM

- Starting a class period with asking a question such as:
  What is something fun you did over the weekend?
  What did you have for breakfast? (Even if they didn't like it, it kept them from starving.)
  What's your favorite movie?
- Include movement breaks, even if it's for one or two minutes.
- Randomly perform the 5-in-10 exercise in whole group discussions or when it would cause the least amount of distraction.
- Pick an ordinary classroom item (a pencil, a paperclip,

a window) and invite students to journal about positive ways it can help them or someone else.

- Challenge students to pick a movie, video game, book, etc. that they do NOT like and list at least three positive things about it. As I mentioned before, I do not like mint-flavored foods, but I appreciate how making mint chocolate chip cookies brings my wife and kids closer together (even though they are totally wasting perfectly good chocolate chip cookies).
- Thank students for sharing questions, answers, and ideas.
- Create thank-you cards for staff on a regular basis. Perhaps randomly pick two or three staff members out of a hat or bowl, and students can pick one to receive a thank-you note for a specific reason. (Depending on the size of your school, you can pull more or fewer names each time).
- Invite students to write thank-you cards to one another for a specific reason. Students can use the Triple A to give them reasons to write. (With the thank-you cards, I advise that you look them over before giving them to recipients.)
- Call or email parents and other caregivers and share your appreciation for how they specifically help your students perform well academically, mentally, and/or socially.
- Recognize students and staff members who achieve success outside the classroom with a card, announcement, or other expression of appreciation. Recognize the tools that brought them that success (the proper mindset, hard work, tenacity, effective time management skills, etc.); perhaps someone else may learn from the high achiever's example. Plus, if

the high achiever is an average or struggling student but an excellent athlete, recognizing the tools they used on the field could translate to them using those tools in the classroom.

- Train students to hold doors for others.
- Go on "pick-up" walks around the school campus and neighborhood (if it's safe to do so), picking up trash and returning school materials to their proper places. Please use safety precautions if necessary, and have students thoroughly wash hands after the walks.
- Create a "How are you doing?" box or send an email with the same subject line, and ask students to respond. Ensure students that their responses are treated with confidentiality, but you will do all that you can to help them if they need assistance.
- Invite students to donate unwanted toys, clothes, and other belongings to local charities during all times of the year.
- Given your comfort level, offer fist bumps/high fives/head nods/other acceptable positive actions to students as they leave your classroom for the day.
- Have short dance parties where you and the students take a mental break from a lesson and move your bodies around. (Note: Given the grade level you teach, this might be an easy sell or just short of pulling teeth. However, if you have fun with it, so will they… eventually.)
- Ask students who compete in competitive activities to discuss lessons they learned from their experiences on the field/stage/court, etc. Reflecting on those experiences not only helps other students understand what their classmates experience, the competing student also increases their own metacognition

(thinking about thinking) skills and even possibly makes those memories richer and more meaningful.

This list is by no means limited to these ideas. We teachers are a creative and innovative lot. In fact, if you have an idea you'd like to share, please message me at @chrisdtgordon or chris@chrisdtgordon.com.

THE TAG JOURNAL

I DESIGNED THE JOURNAL TO help you gain the gratitude benefits I received without spending over two months in the hospital and enduring numerous surgeries. You just think of ONE THING you're thankful for (T), ONE PERSON you appreciate (A), and ONE ACT you can do to make someone else's day better (G).

Psychologists claim that the average person has 6,000 thoughts every day[1]; dedicating three of them to your long-term mental and physical improvement is well worth the effort! What's more, I included 26 weekly journal pages so you can practice for a half-year. I also included a section for you to note your favorite T, A, and G for each week. Additionally, I rotated four areas on which to focus your actions (Family/Close friends, Acquaintances/Colleagues, Community, and Nature) throughout the year. Numerous studies and reports state various lengths of time it takes to establish a habit or routine, most of them much less than 182 days. I want to offer you an opportunity to really ingrain a gratitude practice into your daily life. That even takes into account the chance that you stop practicing but what to come back at some point.

As I am a special education teacher, I am trained to use assessments for data-gathering purposes, and this journal is no exception. However, the data isn't nearly as important for me as it is for you.

Before you start using the journal, you should take the baseline assessment to gauge your current level of gratitude. No matter what your baseline data shows, please remember that this journal is created for you to grow in your gratitude, so there is no such thing as a "bad score." I also created halfway and end-of-journal assessments so you can further gauge your gratitude growth. Something to keep in mind: Progress is RARELY a straight line. Life happens, and your half-year of gratitude might include some really tough patches. Some days might really challenge you to find gratitude, while other days you seem to be basking in grateful glory. That's OK! Stay consistent in your practice, and you will benefit in the long run.

Speaking of challenges, have you ever appreciated a lesson you learned from a challenge or a mistake? I have OH SO MANY examples to choose from personally, but one that sprung to mind as I was writing this section is the wisdom that I've gained from my previous marathon attempts. Had I not learned from those past errors in judgment, I wouldn't be the improved athlete I am now. (It's hard to run double-digit miles on chronically injured legs; trust me on that.) Listing lessons learned in the T section or those who've led you to greater understanding in the A section can offer you loads of options for your daily gratitude practice, and you gain a keener sense of introspection. Win-win!

Finally, if you want to reach out to me and share your data, please feel free to use my various communication modes. It's not necessary by any means, but I'd be pleasantly surprised to hear from you!

WEEKLY JOURNAL PROMPTS

After each week's worth of TAG entries, you will find a page that contains a weekly journal prompt. As the boldfaced words indicate, it's a weekly prompt, which means that you should go back to it throughout the week, maybe a few minutes at a time, to add more thoughts and revelations.

What I really like about these prompts is that some of them aren't about writing. In fact, the first weekly prompt asks you to create a collage of things for which you are grateful. You can draw the items, you can summon your scrapbook skills and clip out pictures out of magazines and other paper-related products, or you can even write the words on the page. It's up to you! No matter the format you use, you are still thinking about those appreciated items, and that's the whole point!

Some of the prompts will seem very simple to you, while others may pose a substantial challenge. Please don't become disheartened if you struggle at times. Out of that struggle will come growth and new insights. No matter what, do your best on these and don't worry about how your talents may stack up to someone else's. This is YOUR journal, not theirs!

THE GRATITUDE LETTER

Like so many areas in life, you can take your gratitude practice to the next level. Writing a detailed gratitude letter to someone who has benefited your life not only lets the recipient know specifically how you feel, but it can also decrease depression levels and possible physical symptoms, such as aches and pains. Over time, practicing gratitude through writing can shift how our brains work so they are rewired in a more positive light[1].

I performed this exercise with Becky. I shared what I appreciated about her as a partner and a mother, and I even shared some self-reflections, especially the ones that have impacted her. She needed to know that I am not ENTIRELY oblivious to how my actions affect her and the kids.

I created 10 letter templates for you to write those detailed letters; they are located after the journal pages. You could also make copies of those sheets so you can share your appreciation with as many people as you wish.

BEFORE YOU START THE JOURNAL

Well, that's all I have for you so far. I will keep challenging myself and growing, so I might create a second edition to this book to update readers on how TAG has positively influenced my life. That's what my mission, my purpose, is all about. Surviving necrotizing fasciitis and all those surgeries was just the beginning. Sure, my loved ones would be OK with me keep on keepin' on, but I wouldn't be. I will keep challenging myself and pushing the envelope as much as I can for as long as I can so I can inspire and motivate others to do the same.

I want you to do that, too. You have more influence than you realize. While many of us suffer from "spotlight syndrome" where we think everyone sees every little mistake we make, people do see how we respond to different situations and what we do with our talents and opportunities. The way you respond to those challenges can help someone shore up the courage to clear their own hurdles. You can be their hero, with or without the cape.

Not only do I hope you use the journal on a daily basis, but I hope you enjoy using it! I always get a kick out of discovering something "new"—something that I've already owned—to appreciate (like the bike stand on my son's mountain bike). Also, observing someone's positive attributes without any connection to me allows me to view them in a different light and appreciate them even more when I realize that we are connected in some way. Finally, I love finding new ways to help other people and give them reasons to be grateful.

If you want to connect with me, whether it's to discuss your TAG journey, to offer me your thoughts about the book, to inquire about how my speaking presentation could impact your school, business, or organization, or just to connect, you can scan the following QR code to find my website, YouTube and podcast channels, and my Facebook, LinkedIn, Instagram pages:

Also, here's my email address again: chris@chrisdtgordon.com

I greatly appreciate you reading this book and learning about my journey and mission. I don't exactly know how it has impacted you, but I hope it has offered you some positivity, hope, motivation, and/or escape from what else you are experiencing. I also hope the journal serves you well so you can serve others well.

With that, I love you, I appreciate you, and I wish nothing but the best for you. Now, get out there, play TAG with everyone you know, and remember to pass on perfection and go for greatness!

ENDNOTES

INTRODUCTION

1. Suma P. Chand, Daniel P. Kuckel , and Martin R. Huecker, "Cognitive Behavior Therapy," *National Library of Medicine*, MY 23, 2023, https://www.ncbi.nlm.nih.gov/books/NBK470241/.

"WHERE YOUR THOUGHTS GO, YOUR MIND AND BODY WILL FOLLOW."

1. Douglas Van Praet. "Watching Food Advertising Seems to Trigger Automatic Eating," *Psychology Today,* July 10, 2021, https://www.psychologytoday.com/us/blog/unconscious-branding/202107/watching-food-advertising-seems-trigger-automatic-eating.
2. Laura M. Miele, PhD. "The Effects of Psychology on Athletic Performance," *Psychology.com*, January 12, 2015, https://www.psychologytoday.com/us/blog/the-whole-athlete/201501/the-effects-psychology-athletic-performance.

3. Phillippa Lally, Cornelia H.M. van Jaarsveld, Henry W.W. Potts, and Jane Wardle, "How are habits formed: Modelling habit formation in the real world," *European Journal of Social Psychology*, Volume 40, Issue 6, p. 998-1009, https://doi.org/10.1002/ejsp.674.

WHAT'S SO SPECIAL ABOUT GRATITUDE?!

1. Robert A. Emmons, Ph. D, *Gratitude Works!*, Jossey-Bass, 2013.

PLAY TAG WITH ME!

1. "How Gratitude Changes You and Your Brain". *Greater Good Magazine.* June 6, 2017, https://greatergood.berkeley.edu/article/item/how_gratitude_changes_you_and_your_brain.

THE TRIPLE A

1. "The Benefits of Helping Others: Improve Your Health Through Good Deeds," Envolve Health, July 6, 2020, https://www.envolvehealth.com/news/the-benefits-of-helping-others--improve-your-health-through-good.html.
2. Jen Gottlieb, *Be Seen*, Hay House, October 30, 2023.

WHAT'S SO SPECIAL ABOUT GRATITUDE?!

1. Viktor Frankl. *Man's Search for Meaning,* Beacon Press, June 1, 2006.

GIVE A LITTLE BIT, GIVE A LITTLE BIT OF YOUR TIME TO OTHERS...

1. Angela Thoreson, L.I.C.S.W., "Helping people, changing lives: 3 health benefits of volunteering," *Mayo Clinic Health System,* August 1, 2023, https://www.mayoclinichealthsystem.org/hometown-health/speaking-of-health/3-health-benefits-of-volunteering.

THE RUNS...NOT THOSE RUNS!

1. Andrew Snow, *Run Elite*, White Tip Publishing, 2023.

BEFORE YOU START THE JOURNAL

1. Jordan Poppenk and Julie Tseng, Brain meta-state transitions demarcate thoughts across task contexts exposing the mental noise of trait neuroticism. *Nature Communications,* Volume 11, Article #3480, July 13, 2020, https://doi.org/10.1038/s41467-020-17255-9.

ABOUT THE AUTHOR

Chris DT Gordon is a veteran online special education teacher and international professional speaker. He holds a master's degree in Special Education (Learning Disabilities), a bachelor's degree in Elementary Education, and four teaching licenses. He also holds a Black Belt from National Taekwondo Institute. He has been speaking since 2020, serving in-person and virtual audiences with his story and message of "The Attitude of Gratitude." Two notable speaking engagements thus far include dressing as One Punch Man to speak at the FanX Convention in Salt Lake City and waking up at 4AM to speaking virtually to Nepalese high school students.

Aside from teaching and speaking, Chris enjoys spending time with his wife Becky and his three kids (Josh, Seth, and Anna), hanging out with his family members and friends, connecting with fellow NF (necrotizing fasciitis) survivors and brothers of Theta Chi Fraternity, training for and running various race distances (like the Boston Marathon), traveling to new places, acting on stage, cosplaying at comic book conventions and for Halloween, watching comic book and science fiction/fantasy movies and shows, waterskiing behind his brother's boat, and receiving dark chocolate and Transformers as gifts. He does not enjoy mint-flavored food (Andes mints are good, though).

THE TAG JOURNAL, ACTUALLY!

TAG BASELINE ASSESSMENT

On a scale of 1 to 5, gauge how often you recognize what you're grateful for.

Using a stopwatch or a clock that counts seconds, count how many things you are grateful for in one minute. Please be honest with your count, as being honest with yourself is the only way to make authentic and lasting change.

1—0-10 things ________ T score________
2—11-20 things ________
3—21-30 things ________
4—31-40 things ________
5—41 or more things ________

On a scale of 1 to 5, gauge the level to which you recognize those around you.

Think about the last week, and count (as accurately as possible) the number of different people you told that you appreciated an action that they did.

Again, please be honest with your count, as being honest with yourself is the only way to make authentic and lasting change.

1—0-5 people ________ A score________
2—6-10 people ________
3—11-15 people ________
4—16-20 people ________
5—41 or more people ________

On a scale of 1 to 5, gauge the level to which you help other people.

Think about the last week, and count (as accurately as possible) the number of times you performed a good deed for another person.

Please be honest with your count, as being honest with yourself is the only way to make authentic and lasting change.

1—0-3 deeds ________ G score________
2—6-10 deeds ________
3—11-15 deeds ________
4—16-20 deeds ________
5—41 or more deeds Total score______

In many assessments, you would add up these scores and I might give you a grade or label. However, the purpose of this journal is to increase your level of gratitude, not to label you. I just want to help you increase your levels of gratitude, happiness, and positive social interaction.

TAG JOURNAL WEEK OF ____________

Family/friends: Who's a family member and a friend who has helped you in the past? Let them know that you still appreciate that kindness.

T: Think about the good things in your life. A: Acknowledge those you appreciate. G: Give others a reason to be grateful.

Su__M__Tu__W__Th__F__Sa__

T:____________________

____

____

A:____________________

____

____

G:____________________

____

____

Su__M__Tu__W__Th__F__Sa__

T:____________________

____

____

A:____________________

____

____

G:____________________

____

____

Su__M__Tu__W__Th__F__Sa__

T:____________________

____

____

A:____________________

____

____

G:____________________

____

____

Su__M__Tu__W__Th__F__Sa__

T:____________________

____

____

A:____________________

____

____

G:____________________

____

____

Su__M__Tu__W__Th__F__Sa__

T:____________________________

____

____

A:____________________________

____

____

G:____________________________

____

____

Su__M__Tu__W__Th__F__Sa__

T:____________________________

____

____

A:____________________________

____

____

G:____________________________

____

____

Su__M__Tu__W__Th__F__Sa__

T:____________________________

____

____

A:____________________________

____

____

G:____________________________

____

____

Favorite TAGs of the week

T:____________________________

____

____

A:____________________________

____

____

G:____________________________

____

____

1 to 3 people I can share TAG with this week:

1.____

2.____

3.____

1. **Gratitude collage:** Create a collage of images or drawings that represent things you're grateful for. Let your creativity flow as you visualize these elements.

TAG JOURNAL WEEK OF ______________

Colleagues: Who's a colleague who has lifted you up when you really needed it? Text them with a thank you this week.

T: Think about the good things in your life. A: Acknowledge those you appreciate. G: Give others a reason to be grateful.

Su__M__Tu__W__Th__F__Sa__

T:______________________________

____

____

A:______________________________

____

____

G:______________________________

____

____

Su__M__Tu__W__Th__F__Sa__

T:______________________________

____

____

A:______________________________

____

____

G:______________________________

____

____

Su__M__Tu__W__Th__F__Sa__

T:______________________________

____

____

A:______________________________

____

____

G:______________________________

____

____

Su__M__Tu__W__Th__F__Sa__

T:______________________________

____

____

A:______________________________

____

____

G:______________________________

____

____

Su__M__Tu__W__Th__F__Sa__

T:____________________________

A:____________________________

G:____________________________

Su__M__Tu__W__Th__F__Sa__

T:____________________________

A:____________________________

G:____________________________

Su__M__Tu__W__Th__F__Sa__

T:____________________________

A:____________________________

G:____________________________

Favorite TAGs of the week

T:____________________________

A:____________________________

G:____________________________

1 to 3 people I can share TAG with this week:

1.____________________________

2.____________________________

3.____________________________

2. **Reverse perspective:** Write about a challenging situation you've faced, and then flip it to find three positive aspects or lessons you've gained from it.

TAG JOURNAL WEEK OF ______________

Community: When out and about, pick up at least 10 pieces of trash this week. Post a picture of you doing it so inspire others to do the same.

T: Think about the good things in your life. A: Acknowledge those you appreciate. G: Give others a reason to be grateful.

Su__M__Tu__W__Th__F__Sa__

T:______________________________

____

____

A:______________________________

____

____

G:______________________________

____

____

Su__M__Tu__W__Th__F__Sa__

T:______________________________

____

____

A:______________________________

____

____

G:______________________________

____

____

Su__M__Tu__W__Th__F__Sa__

T:______________________________

____

____

A:______________________________

____

____

G:______________________________

____

____

Su__M__Tu__W__Th__F__Sa__

T:______________________________

____

____

A:______________________________

____

____

G:______________________________

____

____

Su__M__Tu__W__Th__F__Sa__

T:______________________________
____
____

A:______________________________
____
____

G:______________________________
____
____

Su__M__Tu__W__Th__F__Sa__

T:______________________________
____
____

A:______________________________
____
____

G:______________________________
____
____

Su__M__Tu__W__Th__F__Sa__

T:______________________________
____
____

A:______________________________
____
____

G:______________________________
____
____

Favorite TAGs of the week

T:______________________________
____
____

A:______________________________
____
____

G:______________________________
____
____

1 to 3 people I can share TAG with this week:

1.____
2.____
3.____

3. **Snapshot of joy:** Describe a small moment from today that brought you joy. Capture the scene, your feelings, and why it made you happy.

TAG JOURNAL WEEK OF ______________

Nature: Venture outside at least three times this week. Go different routes. Find one thing to appreciate about each route.

T: Think about the good things in your life. A: Acknowledge those you appreciate. G: Give others a reason to be grateful.

Su__M__Tu__W__Th__F__Sa__

T:______________________________

____

____

A:______________________________

____

____

G:______________________________

____

____

Su__M__Tu__W__Th__F__Sa__

T:______________________________

____

____

A:______________________________

____

____

G:______________________________

____

____

Su__M__Tu__W__Th__F__Sa__

T:______________________________

____

____

A:______________________________

____

____

G:______________________________

____

____

Su__M__Tu__W__Th__F__Sa__

T:______________________________

____

____

A:______________________________

____

____

G:______________________________

____

____

Su__M__Tu__W__Th__F__Sa__

T:______________________________

____

____

A:______________________________

____

____

G:______________________________

____

____

Su__M__Tu__W__Th__F__Sa__

T:______________________________

____

____

A:______________________________

____

____

G:______________________________

____

____

Su__M__Tu__W__Th__F__Sa__

T:______________________________

____

____

A:______________________________

____

____

G:______________________________

____

____

Favorite TAGs of the week

T:______________________________

____

____

A:______________________________

____

____

G:______________________________

____

____

1 to 3 people I can share TAG with this week:

1.______________________________

2.______________________________

3.______________________________

4. **Positivity playlist**: List five songs that always lift your spirits. Explain why each song has a special place in your heart.

TAG JOURNAL WEEK OF ______________

Family/friends: Ask an extended family member about their recent interests (if you don't know); send them a small gift based on said interest.

T: Think about the good things in your life. A: Acknowledge those you appreciate. G: Give others a reason to be grateful.

Su__M__Tu__W__Th__F__Sa__

T:______________________

____

____

A:______________________

____

____

G:______________________

____

____

Su__M__Tu__W__Th__F__Sa__

T:______________________

____

____

A:______________________

____

____

G:______________________

____

____

Su__M__Tu__W__Th__F__Sa__

T:______________________

____

____

A:______________________

____

____

G:______________________

____

____

Su__M__Tu__W__Th__F__Sa__

T:______________________

____

____

A:______________________

____

____

G:______________________

____

____

Su__M__Tu__W__Th__F__Sa__

T:

A:

G:

Su__M__Tu__W__Th__F__Sa__

T:

A:

G:

Su__M__Tu__W__Th__F__Sa__

T:

A:

G:

Favorite TAGs of the week

T:

A:

G:

1 to 3 people I can share TAG with this week:

1.
2.
3.

5. **Kindness chronicle**: Document acts of kindness you've witnessed or experienced recently. Reflect on how these moments have impacted your outlook.

TAG JOURNAL WEEK OF ______________

Colleagues: Text a peer or colleague a reminder about a happy memory that you both share.

T: Think about the good things in your life. A: Acknowledge those you appreciate. G: Give others a reason to be grateful.

Su__M__Tu__W__Th__F__Sa__

T:______________________________

____

____

A:______________________________

____

____

G:______________________________

____

____

Su__M__Tu__W__Th__F__Sa__

T:______________________________

____

____

A:______________________________

____

____

G:______________________________

____

____

Su__M__Tu__W__Th__F__Sa__

T:______________________________

____

____

A:______________________________

____

____

G:______________________________

____

____

Su__M__Tu__W__Th__F__Sa__

T:______________________________

____

____

A:______________________________

____

____

G:______________________________

____

____

Su__M__Tu__W__Th__F__Sa__

T:______________________________
____
____

A:______________________________
____
____

G:______________________________
____
____

Su__M__Tu__W__Th__F__Sa__

T:______________________________
____
____

A:______________________________
____
____

G:______________________________
____
____

Su__M__Tu__W__Th__F__Sa__

T:______________________________
____
____

A:______________________________
____
____

G:______________________________
____
____

Favorite TAGs of the week

T:______________________________
____
____

A:______________________________
____
____

G:______________________________
____
____

1 to 3 people I can share TAG with this week:

1.______________________________

2.______________________________

3.______________________________

6. **Resilience tree**: Draw a tree and its roots. In the roots, jot down challenges you've overcome. In the branches, write accomplishments that have grown from those experiences.

TAG JOURNAL WEEK OF ______________

Community: If you can afford it, buy the purchases of the person behind you in the checkout line of a store.

T: Think about the good things in your life. A: Acknowledge those you appreciate. G: Give others a reason to be grateful.

Su__M__Tu__W__Th__F__Sa__

T:______________________________

____

____

A:______________________________

____

____

G:______________________________

____

____

Su__M__Tu__W__Th__F__Sa__

T:______________________________

____

____

A:______________________________

____

____

G:______________________________

____

____

Su__M__Tu__W__Th__F__Sa__

T:______________________________

____

____

A:______________________________

____

____

G:______________________________

____

____

Su__M__Tu__W__Th__F__Sa__

T:______________________________

____

____

A:______________________________

____

____

G:______________________________

____

____

Su__M__Tu__W__Th__F__Sa__

T:______________________________

____

____

A:______________________________

____

____

G:______________________________

____

____

Su__M__Tu__W__Th__F__Sa__

T:______________________________

____

____

A:______________________________

____

____

G:______________________________

____

____

Su__M__Tu__W__Th__F__Sa__

T:______________________________

____

____

A:______________________________

____

____

G:______________________________

____

____

Favorite TAGs of the week

T:______________________________

____

____

A:______________________________

____

____

G:______________________________

____

____

1 to 3 people I can share TAG with this week:

1.____

2.____

3.____

7. **Grateful for growth:** Write a letter to your past self, expressing gratitude for the challenges that helped you grow into who you are today. Then write a letter to yourself from five years from now, expressing gratitude for the challenges you overcome and the goals you reached.

TAG JOURNAL WEEK OF ______________

Nature: When doing some outside yard work, stretch your rake/shovel a little past your property and help your neighbor (if they would appreciate it).

T: Think about the good things in your life. A: Acknowledge those you appreciate. G: Give others a reason to be grateful.

Su__M__Tu__W__Th__F__Sa__

T:______________________________

____

____

A:______________________________

____

____

G:______________________________

____

____

Su__M__Tu__W__Th__F__Sa__

T:______________________________

____

____

A:______________________________

____

____

G:______________________________

____

____

Su__M__Tu__W__Th__F__Sa__

T:______________________________

____

____

A:______________________________

____

____

G:______________________________

____

____

Su__M__Tu__W__Th__F__Sa__

T:______________________________

____

____

A:______________________________

____

____

G:______________________________

____

____

Su__M__Tu__W__Th__F__Sa__

T:____________________________

____

____

A:____________________________

____

____

G:____________________________

____

____

Su__M__Tu__W__Th__F__Sa__

T:____________________________

____

____

A:____________________________

____

____

G:____________________________

____

____

Su__M__Tu__W__Th__F__Sa__

T:____________________________

____

____

A:____________________________

____

____

G:____________________________

____

____

Favorite TAGs of the week

T:____________________________

____

____

A:____________________________

____

____

G:____________________________

____

____

1 to 3 people I can share TAG with this week:

1.____

2.____

3.____

8. **Three blessings**: List three things you often take for granted and write about why they are blessings in your life.

TAG JOURNAL WEEK OF ______________

Family/friends: Hug every family member/friend you see every day this week (if they are cool with it).

T: Think about the good things in your life. A: Acknowledge those you appreciate. G: Give others a reason to be grateful.

Su__M__Tu__W__Th__F__Sa__

T:______________________________

____

____

A:______________________________

____

____

G:______________________________

____

____

Su__M__Tu__W__Th__F__Sa__

T:______________________________

____

____

A:______________________________

____

____

G:______________________________

____

____

Su__M__Tu__W__Th__F__Sa__

T:______________________________

____

____

A:______________________________

____

____

G:______________________________

____

____

Su__M__Tu__W__Th__F__Sa__

T:______________________________

____

____

A:______________________________

____

____

G:______________________________

____

____

Su__M__Tu__W__Th__F__Sa__

T:______________________________

____

____

A:______________________________

____

____

G:______________________________

____

____

Su__M__Tu__W__Th__F__Sa__

T:______________________________

____

____

A:______________________________

____

____

G:______________________________

____

____

Su__M__Tu__W__Th__F__Sa__

T:______________________________

____

____

A:______________________________

____

____

G:______________________________

____

____

Favorite TAGs of the week

T:______________________________

____

____

A:______________________________

____

____

G:______________________________

____

____

1 to 3 people I can share TAG with this week:

1.____

2.____

3.____

9. **Colorful moments**: Use colors to represent different emotions you've felt today. Explain each color choice and the associated feelings.

TAG JOURNAL WEEK OF ______________

Colleagues: Promote someone else's business on social media.

T: Think about the good things in your life. A: Acknowledge those you appreciate. G: Give others a reason to be grateful.

Su__M__Tu__W__Th__F__Sa__

T:____________________

____

____

A:____________________

____

____

G:____________________

____

____

Su__M__Tu__W__Th__F__Sa__

T:____________________

____

____

A:____________________

____

____

G:____________________

____

____

Su__M__Tu__W__Th__F__Sa__

T:____________________

____

____

A:____________________

____

____

G:____________________

____

____

Su__M__Tu__W__Th__F__Sa__

T:____________________

____

____

A:____________________

____

____

G:____________________

____

____

Su__M__Tu__W__Th__F__Sa__

T:______________________________

____

____

A:______________________________

____

____

G:______________________________

____

____

Su__M__Tu__W__Th__F__Sa__

T:______________________________

____

____

A:______________________________

____

____

G:______________________________

____

____

Su__M__Tu__W__Th__F__Sa__

T:______________________________

____

____

A:______________________________

____

____

G:______________________________

____

____

Favorite TAGs of the week

T:______________________________

____

____

A:______________________________

____

____

G:______________________________

____

____

1 to 3 people I can share TAG with this week:

1.____

2.____

3.____

10. **Unplugged gratitude**: Spend an hour away from screens. Document how you spent your time and how it made you appreciate the present moment.

TAG JOURNAL WEEK OF ______________

Community: Create a positive post about a local business and share it on your socials.

T: Think about the good things in your life. A: Acknowledge those you appreciate. G: Give others a reason to be grateful.

Su__M__Tu__W__Th__F__Sa__

T:______________________________

____

____

A:______________________________

____

____

G:______________________________

____

____

Su__M__Tu__W__Th__F__Sa__

T:______________________________

____

____

A:______________________________

____

____

G:______________________________

____

____

Su__M__Tu__W__Th__F__Sa__

T:______________________________

____

____

A:______________________________

____

____

G:______________________________

____

____

Su__M__Tu__W__Th__F__Sa__

T:______________________________

____

____

A:______________________________

____

____

G:______________________________

____

____

Su__M__Tu__W__Th__F__Sa__

T:______________________________
____
____

A:______________________________
____
____

G:______________________________
____
____

Su__M__Tu__W__Th__F__Sa__

T:______________________________
____
____

A:______________________________
____
____

G:______________________________
____
____

Su__M__Tu__W__Th__F__Sa__

T:______________________________
____
____

A:______________________________
____
____

G:______________________________
____
____

Favorite TAGs of the week

T:______________________________
____
____

A:______________________________
____
____

G:______________________________
____
____

1 to 3 people I can share TAG with this week:

1.______________________________
2.______________________________
3.______________________________

11. **Obstacle course**: Draw a path representing a recent goal you've accomplished. Between the start and finish lines, add obstacles and label them as the various challenges you overcame to reach the finish line. Underneath the course, describe what you needed to do to overcome the obstacles, and what did you learn about yourself in the process.

TAG JOURNAL WEEK OF ______________

Nature: Buy a plant for yourself or someone else.

T: Think about the good things in your life. A: Acknowledge those you appreciate. G: Give others a reason to be grateful.

Su__M__Tu__W__Th__F__Sa__

T:____________________________

____

____

A:____________________________

____

____

G:____________________________

____

____

Su__M__Tu__W__Th__F__Sa__

T:____________________________

____

____

A:____________________________

____

____

G:____________________________

____

____

Su__M__Tu__W__Th__F__Sa__

T:____________________________

____

____

A:____________________________

____

____

G:____________________________

____

____

Su__M__Tu__W__Th__F__Sa__

T:____________________________

____

____

A:____________________________

____

____

G:____________________________

____

____

Su__M__Tu__W__Th__F__Sa__ Su__M__Tu__W__Th__F__Sa__

T:______________________________ T:______________________________

______________________________ ______________________________

______________________________ ______________________________

A:______________________________ A:______________________________

______________________________ ______________________________

______________________________ ______________________________

G:______________________________ G:______________________________

______________________________ ______________________________

______________________________ ______________________________

Su__M__Tu__W__Th__F__Sa__

T:______________________________

____

____

A:______________________________

____

____

G:______________________________

____

____

Favorite TAGs of the week

T:______________________________

____

____

A:______________________________

____

____

G:______________________________

____

____

1 to 3 people I can share TAG with this week:

1.____

2.____

3.____

12. **Nature's beauty**: Take a nature walk or find a scenic spot. Sketch or describe the most beautiful thing you see and reflect on how it makes you feel.

TAG JOURNAL WEEK OF ______________

Family/friends: Do someone else's chore this week; if you don't live with someone else, do a kind act for a stranger.

T: Think about the good things in your life. A: Acknowledge those you appreciate. G: Give others a reason to be grateful.

Su__M__Tu__W__Th__F__Sa__

T:______________________________

____

____

A:______________________________

____

____

G:______________________________

____

____

Su__M__Tu__W__Th__F__Sa__

T:______________________________

____

____

A:______________________________

____

____

G:______________________________

____

____

Su__M__Tu__W__Th__F__Sa__

T:______________________________

____

____

A:______________________________

____

____

G:______________________________

____

____

Su__M__Tu__W__Th__F__Sa__

T:______________________________

____

____

A:______________________________

____

____

G:______________________________

____

____

Su__M__Tu__W__Th__F__Sa__ Su__M__Tu__W__Th__F__Sa__

T:______________________________ T:______________________________

______________________________ ______________________________

______________________________ ______________________________

A:______________________________ A:______________________________

______________________________ ______________________________

______________________________ ______________________________

G:______________________________ G:______________________________

______________________________ ______________________________

______________________________ ______________________________

Su__M__Tu__W__Th__F__Sa__ **Favorite TAGs of the week**

T:______________________________ T:______________________________

______________________________ ______________________________

______________________________ ______________________________

A:______________________________ A:______________________________

______________________________ ______________________________

______________________________ ______________________________

G:______________________________ G:______________________________

______________________________ ______________________________

______________________________ ______________________________

1 to 3 people I can share TAG with this week:

1.____

2.____

3.____

13. **Wise words**: Collect inspiring quotes that resonate with you. Write about how each quote relates to your life and what it teaches you about resilience.

TAG MIDPOINT ASSESSMENT

I hope TAG is treating you well so far!

You have probably noticed that the more you look for things to be thankful for, the easier they are to see, even on tough days.

Keep up the practice!

On a scale of 1 to 5, gauge how often you recognize what you're grateful for.

Using a stopwatch or a clock that counts seconds, count how many things you are grateful for in one minute. Please be honest with your count, as being honest with yourself is the only way to make authentic and lasting change.

1—0-10 things ________ T score________
2—11-20 things ________
3—21-30 things ________
4—31-40 things ________
5—41 or more things ________

On a scale of 1 to 5, gauge the level to which you recognize those around you.

Think about the last week, and count (as accurately as possible) the number of different people you told that you appreciated an action that they did.

Again, please be honest with your count, as being honest with yourself is the only way to make authentic and lasting change.

1—0-5 people	________	A score________
2—6-10 people	________	
3—11-15 people	________	
4—16-20 people	________	
5—41 or more people	________	

On a scale of 1 to 5, gauge the level to which you help other people.

Think about the last week, and count (as accurately as possible) the number of times you performed a good deed for another person.

Please be honest with your count, as being honest with yourself is the only way to make authentic and lasting change.

1—0-3 deeds	________	G score________
2—6-10 deeds	________	
3—11-15 deeds	________	
4—16-20 deeds	________	
5—41 or more deeds		Total score______

No matter what your score is, remember that you are making a difference in the world around you while you are improving yourself.

Reflecting on transformation: Take a moment to consider how far you've come since the beginning of your gratitude journey. Write down three specific instances where your perspective shifted, and you found yourself appreciating something that you might have previously taken for granted. How have these moments of transformation impacted your overall outlook on life?

TAG JOURNAL WEEK OF ______________

Colleagues: Surprise someone you work/volunteer/attend school with by buying them their favorite treat.

T: Think about the good things in your life. A: Acknowledge those you appreciate. G: Give others a reason to be grateful.

Su__M__Tu__W__Th__F__Sa__

T:______________________________
____
____

A:______________________________
____
____

G:______________________________
____
____

Su__M__Tu__W__Th__F__Sa__

T:______________________________
____
____

A:______________________________
____
____

G:______________________________
____
____

Su__M__Tu__W__Th__F__Sa__

T:______________________________
____
____

A:______________________________
____
____

G:______________________________
____
____

Su__M__Tu__W__Th__F__Sa__

T:______________________________
____
____

A:______________________________
____
____

G:______________________________
____
____

Su__M__Tu__W__Th__F__Sa__

T:____________________________
____
____

A:____________________________
____
____

G:____________________________
____
____

Su__M__Tu__W__Th__F__Sa__

T:____________________________
____
____

A:____________________________
____
____

G:____________________________
____
____

Su__M__Tu__W__Th__F__Sa__

T:____________________________
____
____

A:____________________________
____
____

G:____________________________
____
____

Favorite TAGs of the week

T:____________________________
____
____

A:____________________________
____
____

G:____________________________
____
____

1 to 3 people I can share TAG with this week:

1.____
2.____
3.____

14. **Gratitude in silence**: Spend five minutes in quiet meditation. Afterwards, jot down the thoughts and feelings that arose, focusing on the positive and grounding aspects.

TAG JOURNAL WEEK OF ______________

Community: Put away a "misplaced" shopping cart that you find in a store parking lot.

T: Think about the good things in your life. A: Acknowledge those you appreciate. G: Give others a reason to be grateful.

Su__M__Tu__W__Th__F__Sa__

T:______________________

____

____

A:______________________

____

____

G:______________________

____

____

Su__M__Tu__W__Th__F__Sa__

T:______________________

____

____

A:______________________

____

____

G:______________________

____

____

Su__M__Tu__W__Th__F__Sa__

T:______________________

____

____

A:______________________

____

____

G:______________________

____

____

Su__M__Tu__W__Th__F__Sa__

T:______________________

____

____

A:______________________

____

____

G:______________________

____

____

Su__M__Tu__W__Th__F__Sa__

T:______________________________
____
____

A:______________________________
____
____

G:______________________________
____
____

Su__M__Tu__W__Th__F__Sa__

T:______________________________
____
____

A:______________________________
____
____

G:______________________________
____
____

Su__M__Tu__W__Th__F__Sa__

T:______________________________
____
____

A:______________________________
____
____

G:______________________________
____
____

Favorite TAGs of the week

T:______________________________
____
____

A:______________________________
____
____

G:______________________________
____
____

1 to 3 people I can share TAG with this week:

1.____
2.____
3.____

15. **Bucket list sparks**: Write down three adventurous activities you'd like to try someday. Describe how each activity would make you feel, and why you would be grateful for each of them.

TAG JOURNAL WEEK OF ______________

Nature: Visit a park at least once this week (and pick up any garbage you see, please).

T: Think about the good things in your life. A: Acknowledge those you appreciate. G: Give others a reason to be grateful.

Su__M__Tu__W__Th__F__Sa__

T:______________________________

____

____

A:______________________________

____

____

G:______________________________

____

____

Su__M__Tu__W__Th__F__Sa__

T:______________________________

____

____

A:______________________________

____

____

G:______________________________

____

____

Su__M__Tu__W__Th__F__Sa__

T:______________________________

____

____

A:______________________________

____

____

G:______________________________

____

____

Su__M__Tu__W__Th__F__Sa__

T:______________________________

____

____

A:______________________________

____

____

G:______________________________

____

____

Su__M__Tu__W__Th__F__Sa__

T:______________________________
____
____

A:______________________________
____
____

G:______________________________
____
____

Su__M__Tu__W__Th__F__Sa__

T:______________________________
____
____

A:______________________________
____
____

G:______________________________
____
____

Su__M__Tu__W__Th__F__Sa__

T:______________________________
____
____

A:______________________________
____
____

G:______________________________
____
____

Favorite TAGs of the week

T:______________________________
____
____

A:______________________________
____
____

G:______________________________
____
____

1 to 3 people I can share TAG with this week:

1.______________________________

2.______________________________

3.______________________________

16. **Compliment challenge**: Pay a sincere compliment to someone today. Reflect on how both giving and receiving compliments can boost positivity.

TAG JOURNAL WEEK OF ______________

Family/friends: Compliment at least three members of your family or friends this week.

T: Think about the good things in your life. A: Acknowledge those you appreciate. G: Give others a reason to be grateful.

Su__M__Tu__W__Th__F__Sa__

T:____________________

____

____

A:____________________

____

____

G:____________________

____

____

Su__M__Tu__W__Th__F__Sa__

T:____________________

____

____

A:____________________

____

____

G:____________________

____

____

Su__M__Tu__W__Th__F__Sa__

T:____________________

____

____

A:____________________

____

____

G:____________________

____

____

Su__M__Tu__W__Th__F__Sa__

T:____________________

____

____

A:____________________

____

____

G:____________________

____

____

Su__M__Tu__W__Th__F__Sa__

T:____________________________

____

____

A:____________________________

____

____

G:____________________________

____

____

Su__M__Tu__W__Th__F__Sa__

T:____________________________

____

____

A:____________________________

____

____

G:____________________________

____

____

Su__M__Tu__W__Th__F__Sa__

T:____________________________

____

____

A:____________________________

____

____

G:____________________________

____

____

Favorite TAGs of the week

T:____________________________

____

____

A:____________________________

____

____

G:____________________________

____

____

1 to 3 people I can share TAG with this week:

1.____

2.____

3.____

17. **Memory mural**: Create a visual representation of a cherished memory. Include colors, shapes, and symbols that capture the emotions and experiences of that moment.

TAG JOURNAL WEEK OF ______________

Colleagues: Compliment at least five people you work/ attend school/volunteer with this week.

T: Think about the good things in your life. A: Acknowledge those you appreciate. G: Give others a reason to be grateful.

Su__M__Tu__W__Th__F__Sa__

T:____________________________

____

____

A:____________________________

____

____

G:____________________________

____

____

Su__M__Tu__W__Th__F__Sa__

T:____________________________

____

____

A:____________________________

____

____

G:____________________________

____

____

Su__M__Tu__W__Th__F__Sa__

T:____________________________

____

____

A:____________________________

____

____

G:____________________________

____

____

Su__M__Tu__W__Th__F__Sa__

T:____________________________

____

____

A:____________________________

____

____

G:____________________________

____

____

Su__M__Tu__W__Th__F__Sa__

T:______________________________

____

____

A:______________________________

____

____

G:______________________________

____

____

Su__M__Tu__W__Th__F__Sa__

T:______________________________

____

____

A:______________________________

____

____

G:______________________________

____

____

Su__M__Tu__W__Th__F__Sa__

T:______________________________

____

____

A:______________________________

____

____

G:______________________________

____

____

Favorite TAGs of the week

T:______________________________

____

____

A:______________________________

____

____

G:______________________________

____

____

1 to 3 people I can share TAG with this week:

1.____

2.____

3.____

18. **Positivity partner:** Enlist a friend or family member to join you. Share one thing you're grateful for every day, encouraging each other to find the silver lining.

TAG JOURNAL WEEK OF ______________

Community: Compliment at least five people in the community with this week.

T: Think about the good things in your life. A: Acknowledge those you appreciate. G: Give others a reason to be grateful.

Su__M__Tu__W__Th__F__Sa__

T:______________________________

____

____

A:______________________________

____

____

G:______________________________

____

____

Su__M__Tu__W__Th__F__Sa__

T:______________________________

____

____

A:______________________________

____

____

G:______________________________

____

____

Su__M__Tu__W__Th__F__Sa__

T:______________________________

____

____

A:______________________________

____

____

G:______________________________

____

____

Su__M__Tu__W__Th__F__Sa__

T:______________________________

____

____

A:______________________________

____

____

G:______________________________

____

____

Su__M__Tu__W__Th__F__Sa__

T:______________________________

____

____

A:______________________________

____

____

G:______________________________

____

____

Su__M__Tu__W__Th__F__Sa__

T:______________________________

____

____

A:______________________________

____

____

G:______________________________

____

____

Su__M__Tu__W__Th__F__Sa__

T:______________________________

____

____

A:______________________________

____

____

G:______________________________

____

____

Favorite TAGs of the week

T:______________________________

____

____

A:______________________________

____

____

G:______________________________

____

____

1 to 3 people I can share TAG with this week:

1.____

2.____

3.____

19. **Gratitude haiku**: Write a haiku (a three-line poem with 5-7-5 syllable pattern) about something ordinary that you're thankful for.

TAG JOURNAL WEEK OF ______________

Nature: Compliment at least five animals/plants/natural formations/acts of weather this week. (Yes, this has been Compliment Month!)

T: Think about the good things in your life. A: Acknowledge those you appreciate. G: Give others a reason to be grateful.

Su__M__Tu__W__Th__F__Sa__

T:______________________________

____

____

A:______________________________

____

____

G:______________________________

____

____

Su__M__Tu__W__Th__F__Sa__

T:______________________________

____

____

A:______________________________

____

____

G:______________________________

____

____

Su__M__Tu__W__Th__F__Sa__

T:______________________________

____

____

A:______________________________

____

____

G:______________________________

____

____

Su__M__Tu__W__Th__F__Sa__

T:______________________________

____

____

A:______________________________

____

____

G:______________________________

____

____

Su__M__Tu__W__Th__F__Sa__

T:______________________________

____

____

A:______________________________

____

____

G:______________________________

____

____

Su__M__Tu__W__Th__F__Sa__

T:______________________________

____

____

A:______________________________

____

____

G:______________________________

____

____

Su__M__Tu__W__Th__F__Sa__

T:______________________________

____

____

A:______________________________

____

____

G:______________________________

____

____

Favorite TAGs of the week

T:______________________________

____

____

A:______________________________

____

____

G:______________________________

____

____

1 to 3 people I can share TAG with this week:

1.______________________________

2.______________________________

3.______________________________

20. **Adventure awaits:** Plan a dream vacation on paper. Describe the destination, activities, and the excitement you feel about this future adventure.

TAG JOURNAL WEEK OF ______________

Family/friends: Write a kind note for a close family member/friend and place it someplace they'll find it when you're not around.

T: Think about the good things in your life. A: Acknowledge those you appreciate. G: Give others a reason to be grateful.

Su__M__Tu__W__Th__F__Sa__

T:______________________________

____

____

A:______________________________

____

____

G:______________________________

____

____

Su__M__Tu__W__Th__F__Sa__

T:______________________________

____

____

A:______________________________

____

____

G:______________________________

____

____

Su__M__Tu__W__Th__F__Sa__

T:______________________________

____

____

A:______________________________

____

____

G:______________________________

____

____

Su__M__Tu__W__Th__F__Sa__

T:______________________________

____

____

A:______________________________

____

____

G:______________________________

____

____

Su__M__Tu__W__Th__F__Sa__

T:______________________________
____
____

A:______________________________
____
____

G:______________________________
____
____

Su__M__Tu__W__Th__F__Sa__

T:______________________________
____
____

A:______________________________
____
____

G:______________________________
____
____

Su__M__Tu__W__Th__F__Sa__

T:______________________________
____
____

A:______________________________
____
____

G:______________________________
____
____

Favorite TAGs of the week

T:______________________________
____
____

A:______________________________
____
____

G:______________________________
____
____

1 to 3 people I can share TAG with this week:

1.____
2.____
3.____

21. **Daily delight:** Document a small pleasure you enjoyed today, whether it's a delicious meal, a cozy moment, or a soothing aroma.

TAG JOURNAL WEEK OF ______________

Colleagues: Send a kind note to someone who was kind to you years ago, letting them know that act wasn't forgotten.

T: Think about the good things in your life. A: Acknowledge those you appreciate. G: Give others a reason to be grateful.

Su__M__Tu__W__Th__F__Sa__

T:______________________________

____

____

A:______________________________

____

____

G:______________________________

____

____

Su__M__Tu__W__Th__F__Sa__

T:______________________________

____

____

A:______________________________

____

____

G:______________________________

____

____

Su__M__Tu__W__Th__F__Sa__

T:______________________________

____

____

A:______________________________

____

____

G:______________________________

____

____

Su__M__Tu__W__Th__F__Sa__

T:______________________________

____

____

A:______________________________

____

____

G:______________________________

____

____

Su__M__Tu__W__Th__F__Sa__

T:______________________________

____

____

A:______________________________

____

____

G:______________________________

____

____

Su__M__Tu__W__Th__F__Sa__

T:______________________________

____

____

A:______________________________

____

____

G:______________________________

____

____

Su__M__Tu__W__Th__F__Sa__

T:______________________________

____

____

A:______________________________

____

____

G:______________________________

____

____

Favorite TAGs of the week

T:______________________________

____

____

A:______________________________

____

____

G:______________________________

____

____

1 to 3 people I can share TAG with this week:

1.______________________________

2.______________________________

3.______________________________

22. **Character strength:** List three personal strengths you possess. Describe how these strengths have helped you navigate challenges and achieve your goals.

TAG JOURNAL WEEK OF ____________

Community: Hold the door for at least 10 different people this week.

T: Think about the good things in your life. A: Acknowledge those you appreciate. G: Give others a reason to be grateful.

Su__M__Tu__W__Th__F__Sa__

T:________________________

____

____

A:________________________

____

____

G:________________________

____

____

Su__M__Tu__W__Th__F__Sa__

T:________________________

____

____

A:________________________

____

____

G:________________________

____

____

Su__M__Tu__W__Th__F__Sa__

T:________________________

____

____

A:________________________

____

____

G:________________________

____

____

Su__M__Tu__W__Th__F__Sa__

T:________________________

____

____

A:________________________

____

____

G:________________________

____

____

Su__M__Tu__W__Th__F__Sa__

T:________________________________

____

____

A:________________________________

____

____

G:________________________________

____

____

Su__M__Tu__W__Th__F__Sa__

T:________________________________

____

____

A:________________________________

____

____

G:________________________________

____

____

Su__M__Tu__W__Th__F__Sa__

T:________________________________

____

____

A:________________________________

____

____

G:________________________________

____

____

Favorite TAGs of the week

T:________________________________

____

____

A:________________________________

____

____

G:________________________________

____

____

1 to 3 people I can share TAG with this week:

1.____

2.____

3.____

23. **Comfort corner:** Create a cozy space in your journal dedicated to things that bring you comfort—favorite quotes, doodles, and mementos.

TAG JOURNAL WEEK OF ______________

Nature: Offer to mow your neighbor's lawn or shovel their driveway/walkways.

T: Think about the good things in your life. A: Acknowledge those you appreciate. G: Give others a reason to be grateful.

Su__M__Tu__W__Th__F__Sa__

T:____________________________

____

____

A:____________________________

____

____

G:____________________________

____

____

Su__M__Tu__W__Th__F__Sa__

T:____________________________

____

____

A:____________________________

____

____

G:____________________________

____

____

Su__M__Tu__W__Th__F__Sa__

T:____________________________

____

____

A:____________________________

____

____

G:____________________________

____

____

Su__M__Tu__W__Th__F__Sa__

T:____________________________

____

____

A:____________________________

____

____

G:____________________________

____

____

Su__M__Tu__W__Th__F__Sa__

T:______________________________
____
____

A:______________________________
____
____

G:______________________________
____
____

Su__M__Tu__W__Th__F__Sa__

T:______________________________
____
____

A:______________________________
____
____

G:______________________________
____
____

Su__M__Tu__W__Th__F__Sa__

T:______________________________
____
____

A:______________________________
____
____

G:______________________________
____
____

Favorite TAGs of the week

T:______________________________
____
____

A:______________________________
____
____

G:______________________________
____
____

1 to 3 people I can share TAG with this week:

1.______________________________
2.______________________________
3.______________________________

24. **Gratitude snapshot:** Take a photo of something you appreciate, print it, and stick it in your journal. Write about why that image sparks gratitude.

TAG JOURNAL WEEK OF ______________

Family/friends: Ask each person you live with or are close to how they are doing (and ask follow-up questions) this week.

T: Think about the good things in your life. A: Acknowledge those you appreciate. G: Give others a reason to be grateful.

Su__M__Tu__W__Th__F__Sa__

T:______________________________

____

____

A:______________________________

____

____

G:______________________________

____

____

Su__M__Tu__W__Th__F__Sa__

T:______________________________

____

____

A:______________________________

____

____

G:______________________________

____

____

Su__M__Tu__W__Th__F__Sa__

T:______________________________

____

____

A:______________________________

____

____

G:______________________________

____

____

Su__M__Tu__W__Th__F__Sa__

T:______________________________

____

____

A:______________________________

____

____

G:______________________________

____

____

Su__M__Tu__W__Th__F__Sa__

T:__________

A:__________

G:__________

Su__M__Tu__W__Th__F__Sa__

T:__________

A:__________

G:__________

Su__M__Tu__W__Th__F__Sa__

T:__________

A:__________

G:__________

Favorite TAGs of the week

T:__________

A:__________

G:__________

1 to 3 people I can share TAG with this week:

1.__________

2.__________

3.__________

25. **Observe and reflect:** Find a quiet place and observe your surroundings for a few minutes. Record the beauty and details you notice, cultivating mindfulness and positivity.

TAG JOURNAL WEEK OF ______________

Colleagues/Community/Nature: Play a fun game with a peer or colleague of their choice outside in a public place (if the weather permits).

T: Think about the good things in your life. A: Acknowledge those you appreciate. G: Give others a reason to be grateful.

Su__M__Tu__W__Th__F__Sa__

T:______________________________
____
____
A:______________________________
____
____
G:______________________________
____
____

Su__M__Tu__W__Th__F__Sa__

T:______________________________
____
____
A:______________________________
____
____
G:______________________________
____
____

Su__M__Tu__W__Th__F__Sa__

T:______________________________
____
____
A:______________________________
____
____
G:______________________________
____
____

Su__M__Tu__W__Th__F__Sa__

T:______________________________
____
____
A:______________________________
____
____
G:______________________________
____
____

Su__M__Tu__W__Th__F__Sa__

T:________________________________

A:________________________________

G:________________________________

Su__M__Tu__W__Th__F__Sa__

T:________________________________

A:________________________________

G:________________________________

Su__M__Tu__W__Th__F__Sa__

T:________________________________

A:________________________________

G:________________________________

Favorite TAGs of the week

T:________________________________

A:________________________________

G:________________________________

1 to 3 people I can share TAG with this week:

1.____

2.____

3.____

26. **Hopeful horizon:** Draw a sunrise over the horizon. Write about the new opportunities and blessings you're looking forward to in the days ahead.

TAG FINAL ASSESSMENT

On a scale of 1 to 5, gauge how often you recognize what you're grateful for.

Using a stopwatch or a clock that counts seconds, count how many things you are grateful for in one minute. Please be honest with your count, as being honest with yourself is the only way to make authentic and lasting change.

1—0-10 things	________	T score________
2—11-20 things	________	
3—21-30 things	________	
4—31-40 things	________	
5—41 or more things	________	

On a scale of 1 to 5, gauge the level to which you recognize those around you.

Think about the last week, and count (as accurately as possible) the number of different people you told that you appreciated an action that they did.

Again, please be honest with your count, as being honest with yourself is the only way to make authentic and lasting change.

1—0-5 people	________	A score________
2—6-10 people	________	
3—11-15 people	________	
4—16-20 people	________	
5—41 or more people	________	

On a scale of 1 to 5, gauge the level to which you help other people.

Think about the last week, and count (as accurately as possible) the number of times you performed a good deed for another person.

Please be honest with your count, as being honest with yourself is the only way to make authentic and lasting change.

1—0-3 deeds	_______	G score_______
2—6-10 deeds	_______	
3—11-15 deeds	_______	
4—16-20 deeds	_______	
5—41 or more deeds		Total score_____

Thank you so much for playing TAG for six months!

It is my hope, my dream, my aspiration that you have grown and increased your gratitude, positivity, and resilience so much that you have inspired others to do the same. Remember to use the following pages to send gratitude letters to important people in your life. Please keeping playing TAG and be the hero the world needs you to be!

Now, pass on perfection and go for greatness!

Dear______________________________

Dear_______________________________

Dear______________________________

Dear______________________________

Dear______________________________

Dear______________________________

Dear______________________________

Dear______________________________

Dear______________________________

Dear______________________________

Made in the USA
Middletown, DE
25 August 2024

59170197R00130